The Truth about Medical Malpractice

The Truth about Medical Malpractice

The Patient's Rights

The Doctor's Rights

Ronald E. Gots, M.D., Ph.D.

STEIN AND DAY *Publishers*/New York

First published in 1975

Designed by Ed Kaplin
Printed in the United States of America
Stein and Day/*Publishers*/Scarborough House,
Briarcliff Manor, N.Y. 10510

SECOND PRINTING 1976

Library of Congress Cataloging in Publication Data

Gots, Ronald E
The truth about medical malpractice.

1. Malpractice—United States. I. Title.
KF1289.G63 346'.73'033 75-11801
ISBN 0-8128-1831-8

Dedication

To my family: Barbara, Jason, Selma, Joe and Lynne

To my friends: Steve, Bill, and Janice

The case studies in this book are true, but the names, places, and particulars have been changed to preserve the privacy of those involved.

Contents

Who's to Blame?

As Dr. Lerner wearily walked out of the hospital to his car, his last surgical patient was the object of concerned activity in the recovery room. Her seven-pound newborn son had emerged from the Cesarean section unscathed and was resting comfortably in the nursery. His mother was just awakening from the ordeal. Childbirth, normally so simple, for Linda Smullen was to be disastrous.

Linda's Cesarean section was complicated by massive bleeding. Instead of fully separating from the uterine wall, as usually occurs, her placenta was deeply imbedded in the substance of the womb itself. Dr. Lerner, faced with this potentially fatal situation, made a poor decision. Removing the bleeding uterus was mandatory. He left it in hoping that the bleeding would stop. By the time Dr. Lerner pulled out of the hospital driveway, the seventh unit of blood slowly dripped into Linda's vein.

It was 8:30 when Dr. Lerner opened his front door. He was greeted by the familiar, unwelcome sound of a ringing phone. The deep concern evident in the anxious report of the recovery room nurse failed to activate the exhausted gynecologist.

"Start the eighth unit of blood. As long as her blood pressure is holding at ninety, I think we'll be okay."

Hour after hour this scenario was repeated; first the call, then the order, "More blood."

Finally, at midnight, following the infusion of the fifteenth unit, the nurse was insistent. "Doctor, I think you'd better come in. Mrs. Smullen's blood pressure is still falling."

Dr. Lerner mumbled some profanities to himself as he drove towards the hospital for the fourth night in a row. Images of his comfortable bed kept intruding into his fatigued mind. "Why the hell did I ever go into medicine anyway?" he thought.

Moments after his arrival he was rushing this critically ill woman to the operating room. A belated hysterectomy averted immediate death, but the delay proved too much for Linda. The prolonged shock and fifteen blood transfusions were more than her body could tolerate. She died four days later.

Dr. Lerner's grave error—a poor operative decision compounded by later inaction—cost this young woman her life. His malpractice was as fatal as an assailant's bullet.

Dr. Kirkland brought his thumbs together to flatten the second loop of the square knot. The last skin suture was firmly in place, ending the appendectomy.

Twelve-year-old Billie Martin, who had just this morning played a rough and tumble game of football, tonight lay motionless in the recovery room bed. If everything went as expected he would be home in six days. After all, this was a "simple" operation. The appendix hadn't ruptured, and there were no apparent complications.

But Billie failed to improve in the predicted manner. Two days after the operation his temperature shot up to 103 degrees. He could no longer eat and was vomiting. His abdomen became firm and silent—cardinal signs of peritonitis.

The surgical team responded quickly. They introduced large doses of well-chosen antibiotics into Billie's veins, infused copious quantities of intravenous fluids, and provided the best supportive care that modern medicine could offer. For some unexplainable reason, Billie failed to respond. Despite their diligence, despite the fact that this was the modern era of medical miracles, despite all the wonder drugs, their efforts were futile. Billie's infection spread relentlessly. His kidneys failed; he slipped into coma and he died.

To the grief-stricken parents this had to be malpractice. Somehow the doctors rather than nature must have been at fault. Could this happen without malpractice? A normal boy fatally stricken by a postoperative infection? Yes, indeed! In this case, Billie's care had been excellent, yet his infection could not be halted. Though the result was tragic, there was no malpractice.

"All she needs is a shot of penicillin!"

Dr. London, not wanting to appear impotent or uncooperative, nodded his head at the imploring mother. He knew that penicillin couldn't help four-year-old Joyce's cold, but if it made the mother feel better, why not?

Ten minutes after the nurse withdrew the needle from the arm of the screaming child, the youngster clutched her throat and gasped for air. An allergic reaction to the antibiotic, unusual, but by no means rare, had constricted her throat, depriving her body of essential oxygen. The mother, panic-stricken, made an illegal U-turn and pushed the accelerator pedal to the floor. Within three minutes she was back in the doctor's office, her ashen child in her arms. Emergency resuscitation was to no avail. The child could not be revived.

Because he gave an unnecessary drug, the doctor was negligent. That negligence was the direct cause of a child's death. True, the mother had requested the penicillin shot, but the final decision was a medical one. It was the doctor's responsibility to deny the request for improper treatment. He failed in that responsibility.

The driver of the rescue vehicle skidded on the damp asphalt and nearly caused another accident in his haste to reach the hospital. His battered passenger, a prominent architect, lay, still unconscious, in the back.

He awoke in the hospital, stunned, confused, but happy to be alive. It wasn't until the resident physician completed his evaluation that the dreadful reality unfolded. Every muscle from the neck down was immobile, disobeying his mind's command to move. He was paralyzed!

The first weeks in the hospital would be the most telling prognostically. Significant improvement meant a good chance for recovery; little change meant recovery was unlikely. For this hapless man, his family and the attending neurosurgeon, that week seemed interminable.

By the end of three weeks, all evidence of improvement had ceased entirely. This man, once a distinguished and vital individual, lay helplessly in his bed. The neurosurgeon, now certain of the poor prognosis, conferred with his patient and the family. An exploratory operation in his neck, although quite likely to be unsuccessful, was the last remaining thread of hope.

The surgeon's knife gently parted the delicate tissues that overlay the spinal cord. As the fluid-filled spinal canal and the gray-white cord that carries its tiny nerve fibers came into view, the neurosurgeon's hope was shattered. There was no evidence of obstruction or pressure that might be relieved by his skillful manipulations. His patient's paralysis was due to severe destruction of the cord itself. The operation was bound to fail.

Several hours later his patient awoke. He commanded his body to move: no response. The left leg: nothing. Now the right hand and leg: nothing here either. Even those small movements he could make before the operation were now gone. Hope abruptly changed to despair. His last chance —the operation—was a dismal failure. Now he knew that he would live out his days a cripple.

The inevitable period of self-pity and "why me" questions gradually gave way to hostile recriminations. First, against the reckless teenaged driver who had destroyed his body. Then, against the doctor whose operation, once the source of great hope, had failed to cure him and even seemed to make him worse. Day by day, his anger grew until he felt certain that the doctor, through some grievous error, had sealed his miserable fate. Shortly before he entered a rehabilitation hospital for prolonged care, he reached a firm decision—he would sue the doctor.

The preparation for the suit and the heated courtroom battle will be described in a later chapter. But to understand the basis for this and the preceding cases, we must first lay the groundwork. What is malpractice? What are patients' rights? What are doctors' rights? Why do patients sue their doctors? How is malpractice and malpractice litigation shattering the very foundations of American medical practice? These vital issues will be explored in the chapters that follow. Once we gain some understanding of malpractice and malpractice suits, we can share the experience of our paralyzed architect and other distraught patients as they seek redress, justified or misguided, against their doctors.

1

The Birth of a Suit

Sue Dr. Welby? His patients wouldn't dream of it! The fatherly family practitioner may never have to defend himself in court. It is not that he never makes mistakes—even the best physician cannot practice for thirty years without accidentally harming a patient through improper management. But Dr. Welby's mistakes don't lead to suits. Why not?

Before a suit is filed the patient must accept the idea of suing, and he must have a provocation. The acceptance may stem from lack of confidence in his doctor or from a distrust of doctors in general. The provocation arises from a specific event which the patient construes as negligent: ineffective treatment of a disease, a too-high medical bill, or a physician's arrogance or rudeness.

The disgruntled patient who is angry at physicians in general and his own in particular may sue over a minor incident. Dr. Welby's fictional patient, on the other hand, who is deeply involved with his physician, would demand clear evidence of negligence and a major, possibly devastating, complication before he would consider suing.

Very few Dr. Welbys survive in our modern era of specialized medicine. With the loss of the respected family practitioner, people's willingness to overlook errors in diagnosis and treatment has also waned. An acceptance of suing, the first element in malpractice suits, has escalated.

Recent social changes and advances in medical technology have eroded the doctor-patient relationship, and doctors are at least partially responsible. Relying more and more on complex technology, doctors have largely forgotten the art of medicine and of dealing with patients. At the same time they have fallen victim to an arrogance of power and prestige, which has infuriated a public just becoming aware of its rights as consumers.

At the turn of the century American physicians enjoyed respect and social prominence. The physician was far more effective in dealing with disease than he had been just a generation earlier. Specialization was limited, and the family doctor treated not just individuals but whole families, sometimes from birth to death; he was doctor, confidant, and counselor.

During the first half of the twentieth century, modern instrumentation, new insights into disease processes, and miracle drugs markedly enhanced effective therapy. As medicine shifted from an art to a scientific practice, the ties between doctors and their patients weakened. Whereas earlier physicians, who had at their disposal few scientific methods, relied largely on close personal interactions with their patients and in individualized therapy, modern physicians could write a prescription and let the penicillin do the trick. It became both easier and more efficient to order a battery of laboratory studies and see the patient later, results in hand. Interviewing the patient and performing a comprehensive physical examination, while still important, took a back seat to the X-ray reports and laboratory computer printouts.

Finally, the burgeoning scientific revolution placed the wide scope of medicine beyond the reach of a single practitioner. Radiology, ophthalmology, pediatrics, orthopedics, and dermatology each developed a voluminous system of knowledge and skills. The growth of specialties further isolated the doctor from sick people. Rarely seeing a patient for more than a brief consultation, a specified course of therapy, or a surgical procedure, the specialist is only a transient participant in the patient's path to recovery. An operation takes only a few hours, while a foundation of trust takes much longer to establish.

Scientific medicine, with its armamentarium of sophisticated laboratory tests, diagnostic tools, and the most advanced drugs, both improved the health of the public and destroyed the reverence it held for the doctor. The degree of respect that did remain has been largely undermined in the past twenty years by physicians themselves.

In 1900 the family practitioner would have treated Mr. Jones for an infection in his lung. His modern counterpart focuses on the X ray, which shows the disease to be a pneumonia. Cultures, carefully and correctly taken, will identify the causative organism. Sophisticated tests result in the correct diagnosis and treatment, but Mr. Jones—the suffering human being—can easily become lost in the shuffle. The contemporary physician is more successful, but the cost of scientific sophistication has been great. By treating the disease rather than the sick person, by interposing the specialist between the primary physician and his patient, doctors have contributed to the erosion of the position and respect accorded them by society.

Another undesirable side effect of modern medicine was the gradual emergence of a subtle but definite change in physician attitudes.

At first modern medical advances enhanced the physician's prestige, for the marvelous new techniques grew up in the shadow of the revered family practitioner. Physicians responded, humanly, by looking upon themselves with the same sense of importance accorded them by the community. They became inflexible in their approach to patients, believing themselves to be omniscient. They demanded blind compliance with their recommendations and complete acceptance of their advice. The prevalent feeling in the medical community was that patients, who had no understanding of the complexities of medicine, did not require explanations.

Thus, modern skills added both a new dimension to medical practice and a sense of arrogance, elitism, and an inflated concept of the capabilities of medicine. The patient, as a person with needs, desires, and problems, as well as a disease, was forgotten. Patients' concerns, fears, and complaints became secondary to their chest X rays and blood counts.

Earlier physicians knew their limitations and therefore received complaints sympathetically even if they could detect no abnormalities. The expectations of modern physicians grew more rapidly than their diagnostic capabilities. Reliance on laboratory reports has become so firm that physicians succumb to the temptation of dismissing a complaint that cannot be explained by an X-ray finding or a blood abnormality.

But modern methods are still limited: doubtless many diseases are still undetectable by modern laboratory and X-ray techniques. Yet today the not uncommon patient whose illness resists laboratory diagnosis is too often brushed aside or sent for psychotherapy.

Finally, the doctor-patient relationship has been strained by new pressures on the doctor's time. Unequal distribution of medical practitioners and social programs that have made health care available for almost all of our citizens have filled doctors' offices to overflowing.

For the same reasons, house calls have become obsolete. They represent an inefficient form of medical care, since the doctor can see ten patients in his office in the time required for a house call. Home visits are also ineffective, because equipment and facilities which are often needed are available only in the doctor's office or in the hospital. Despite justifications, the public has viewed the demise of the house call as additional evidence of the callous impersonality of modern medicine.

Fifty years ago the public might have accepted an authoritative and condescending attitude from the family practitioner. Today it will not. No longer will people stand being patted on the head and told to have faith in their physician, who, of course, knows what is best. Consumer groups, magazine articles, and television specials have all focused on the quality of health-care delivery and the competence of physicians. People are now aware of the fact that not all doctors are equally qualified or capable. They compare, question, and become more personally involved in all aspects of their medical care. They want to know why a procedure is being undertaken, what the alternatives are, and what the risks and complications might be. Patients have a desire for and a right to this information, but their questioning has forcefully clashed with the physician's concepts of his prerogatives. The striking rise in malpractice claims provides graphic testimony to this conflict of interests.

The proliferation of lawsuits, therefore, is largely a response to the loss of the art of medicine, the advances in scientific medical practices, ever-increasing specialization, and patients' new awareness of their rights. All of these are social factors that relate to the ways in which patients view their physicians and physicians deal with their patients.

Does more malpractice occur now than in 1900? The answer is undoubtedly yes, but it does not represent an indictment of the modern physician. As technology improves and the physician is able to do more, his responsibilities and opportunities for error increase proportionately. The turn-of-the-century physician could not have been expected to diagnose the pneumonia accurately, since the X-ray machine had not been invented. But woe to his modern counterpart who misses the diagnosis because he failed to order an X ray!

Thus, changing attitudes by physicians and society have progressively laid the groundwork for the increase in malpractice suits. Yet the fact remains that not everybody sues his physician. Certain specific motivations must drive one to the courtroom door.

Millie knew that her stomach problems were not just in her head. That miserable gnawing feeling in her abdomen, the frequent bouts of watery diarrhea, the belly cramps and occasional vomiting—something must be wrong inside. She had seen ten doctors in five years. Most of them were specialists. Six barium enema studies and seven upper gastrointestinal X rays later, the answer was still the same: no visible disease.

Each of the specialists confronted Millie with the same

repetitious diagnosis: like many people, Millie vented her worries and anxieties through her gastrointestinal tract. She was not "crazy," and her symptoms were not imaginary. Had they been caused by an ulcer, they could not have been more real or distressing. However, therapy for her "nervous stomach" was less specific and much less promising than treatment for an ulcer. Her only recourses were tranquilizers, sedatives, bowel relaxants, and possibly psychotherapy.

Of the ten physicians who cared for her, some were compassionate while others were cold. Three had spent a great deal of time and effort trying to help Millie understand and cope emotionally with her debilitating problem. Others had appeared less concerned, and two had been excessively curt and, as far as Millie was concerned, downright rude. To them Millie represented one of hundreds of similar patients with complaints but no demonstrable disease—a frustrating experience for a physician who prefers clear-cut diagnoses and treatment. Distressed by the lack of a curable problem, such physicians subconsciously find a common remedy: rejection of the patient.

Millie became convinced that all of her doctors had been wrong, and she resolved to sue each one of them. She found a young attorney with limited malpractice experience who took the case and began reviewing her voluminous records and searching for medical experts. After two years of intensive investigation, costing $3,000 of Millie's retirement savings, she was forced to drop the case. Every expert had reached the same conclusion: the physician defendants had done everything medically possible to help her.

Millie suffered from a chronic disease resistant to modern therapy. The anguish of that realization or the desire to deny that possibility is a frequent motivation for malpractice litigation. It is an understandable feeling that "it can't be so," and therefore that the doctor must be wrong.

"That damned foot still hurts, and it's getting worse," thought Leo. "Those doctors aren't helping. I don't think they know what they're doing." If it were not for the fact that Leo's oldest son was an M.D., he probably would have sued the last three physicians who had cared for him.

Leo had a chronic, hard-to-treat complication of hardening of the arteries. He suffered from constant pains in his foot and leg, and he was unable to find reassurance from his busy physicians. An operation on his arteries was indicated, but Leo faced a fifty-fifty chance of improving and a 10 percent chance of dying as a result of the operation. Instead of carefully and compassionately explaining the risks and benefits, Dr. L., the vascular surgeon responded curtly to the patient's anxious questioning. "Do you think my pain will be better after the operation?" Leo asked. "Your guess is as good as mine, " snapped the physician. Leo decided against the operation.

Fortunately, Leo's son knew that surgical correction, although risky, was his father's only hope for a productive, pain-free life. He painstakingly explained the procedure, emphasizing the potential benefit without minimizing the possible dangers, and Leo agreed to the operation.

He was admitted to a large New York hospital, the teaching center for a major medical school. Upon arriving he was greeted by a third-year medical student, whose inexperience and desire to be thorough led to a three-hour history and physical examination. Next came the intern. He was more hurried and spent only one hour, but he repeated the same questions and listened to the same places with his stethoscope. Then arrived the first-year resident and the chief resident. Again the same questions. By the time he saw his surgeon, Dr. L., Leo was furious. He had been hammered, poked, pushed, and listened to by four strange physicians before even seeing his own doctor.

Dr. L. did little to comfort Leo or to allay his fury. "Your son's a doctor, and you should know what happens in a teaching hospital. If you don't want to be examined by lots of doctors, you shouldn't have come to a university hospital."

Leo was ready to walk out. "The hell with the operation." He was dressed and his bags were packed when his son arrived and convinced him to stay.

The operation and immediate postoperative period went smoothly. On the fifth day he developed an infection in the operative incision. The intern first thought he spotted an infection, but the resident disagreed. The chief resident was not sure. The medical student wanted to open and drain the incision. Leo's head was spinning with confusion, certain that he was being dangerously victimized by a group of incompetent physicians.

Actually, all of their viewpoints were justified, since the diagnosis of a wound infection was hard to make, but their lack of communication with each other and with Leo gave the impression of utter confusion. Fortunately, the infection was properly treated, and Leo recovered uneventfully, but his experiences in the hospital destroyed his faith in physicians.

Leo's case illustrates several important points. Since the operation was successful and correctly performed he had no grounds for a suit, but he had plenty of reason to be angry. His surgeon was rude and unwilling to take the time to answer questions and develop a trusting relationship. Leo was unprepared for the extensive examinations by a multitude of physicians (he probably would have enjoyed all the interest shown in him had he been forewarned). Finally, the four doctors who evaluated his postoperative problem should have conferred, discussed the problem together, and jointly presented their consensus to Leo instead of upsetting him by disagreeing in front of him. Through their combined hurried behavior, all of the physicians involved antagonized Leo. It would require only a small act of medical negligence in the future to enrage Leo enough to bring a suit.

The individuals just described—Millie and Leo—suffered from chronic illnesses that crippled their day-to-day living. Their typical feelings of despair and anger give rise to most malpractice suits, and many court battles could be avoided if physicians were to take the time to develop a foundation of trust. The patient would be more inclined to accept his chronic problem, and he would be less apt to sue the practitioner whose kind and patient words helped him through his emotional stress. A patient who understands his disease and accepts the diagnostic and therapeutic regimen which he and his doctor have discussed together is unlikely to feel totally helpless and frustrated by the cold, complex medical scene.

While emotional responses trigger malpractice suits, these are often without medical or legal merit. Consequently, 50 percent of all malpractice complaints never become suits, and of those that do, 75 percent are won by the defending physicians. Futile lawsuits are expensive for plaintiffs and defendants and emotionally draining as well. For this reason the concerned patient, contemplating a lawsuit, must attempt to differentiate between a valid and a frivolous claim.

Even before a lawyer is contacted, several questions should be posed. First, what is the reason for the suit? The only valid justification is a specific, injurious error made by the physician. An unpleasant or rude doctor gives one ample reason to look for a new practitioner, but these personal traits alone are not grounds for a lawsuit. An excessive bill may be grounds for a complaint to the local medical society, but not reason to sue. A poor prognosis or slow progress, on the other hand, might justify a suit if either resulted from physician error. A vast number of diseases are not amenable to therapy, and, no matter how disturbing that realization may be to a patient, it does not provide the basis for a lawsuit. One must, therefore, ask whether several physicians concurred with the diagnosis, or whether one came up with a more beneficial treatment or clearer answer. If a number of doctors all offer the same bad news, as was the case with Millie, there is reason to believe that the problem is one which defies treatment.

Asking these simple questions and honestly evaluating the answers will reduce the likelihood of pursuing an expensive, emotionally traumatic, and losing lawsuit. If the determination to file a suit remains, there are two more crucial questions to answer. First, did some treatment—surgery, a drug, an office procedure—produce an unexpected and serious complication? Second, did another doctor find a previous physician's error, an error that led to a physical injury or a significant hardship?

B.L. suffered frequent bouts of watery diarrhea and abdominal pain. She saw her physician, a compassionate, elderly general practitioner, who reassured her, gave her some bowel-relaxing medicine, and made an appointment for six months later. The medication improved the symptoms somewhat, but they persisted.

B.L. complained again, and the doctor again reassured her. "People's nerves frequently give rise to intestinal symptoms." This information was particularly appropriate for B.L., the first female bank executive in her city. The pressures on her were enormous, and she had every reason to have a "nervous stomach." She willingly accepted the diagnosis.

Finally, after two years of intermittent discomfort and frequent visits to her physician, B.L. demanded a more complete evaluation. She saw a local internist, who ordered a number of tests, including a barium X ray of her intestinal tract. It revealed a shocking finding: a tumor, probably malignant, in the large intestine. An operation was performed, but it was too late. The cancer had spread to her liver. The two-year delay in the diagnosis probably had contributed to the spread. B.L. sued the general practitioner and received a large out-of-court settlement.

In this case B.L. had been treated compassionately. She was not upset with her physician's manner, but rather with his failure to diagnose her condition. She was clearly the victim of a physician's error, which was uncovered by a second doctor.

A significant and unexpected complication or a demonstrated injurious error may indicate malpractice. Neither automatically proves mismanagement, since complications and errors in diagnosis can occur under the best circumstances. However, in the absence of such a complication or error a malpractice claim will be hard to support.

These, then, are general guidelines for the unhappy patient considering a suit: Evaluate the role of emotional factors in the decision. Dissatisfaction with one's medical progress or dislike of the physician without specific acts of wrongdoing leads to expensive losing suits. Specific unexpected injuries or documented errors in diagnosis, on the other hand, may be grounds for a valid claim.

2

The Anatomy of a Malpractice Case

Malpractice, or a malpractice case? There is a wide gap between the two. Each of us has violated a traffic rule without causing an accident, and all basketball fans know the slogan "No harm, no foul"—implying that a flagrant violation may be overlooked if it does not interfere with the game. The same holds true in medicine. Mistakes are made every day without causing any harm. Those errors constitute malpractice, but they cannot stand alone as the basis of a lawsuit.

When can medical malpractice lead to a suit? Just as the reckless driver will find himself in a court after he destroys a pole or has a collision with another automobile, so too will the physician be liable when his carelessness causes a patient harm. Further, there must be a clear link between the act of negligence and the resulting injury. This requirement, known as proximate cause, bridges the gap between malpractice and a malpractice case. It says, "You, Doctor, through carelessness or negligence, directly caused the patient harm."

Injury, negligence, and proximate cause are the three fundamental elements that determine a malpractice case. Understanding the basic features of each may help the disgruntled patient contemplating a lawsuit to better appreciate his legal position.

INJURY

A necessary requirement for a medical malpractice case is a concrete, definable injury. An operative complication, a serious drug side effect, an unusually prolonged hospitalization, an unexpected death, the loss of a limb from a seemingly minor injury, may or may not lead to successful court action. Unexpected complications like these can occur despite careful medical treatment. However, such complications can also follow a medical error. If so, the injured patient may have cause for a valid lawsuit.

Injuries can take many forms: from evident physical impairments to loss of life; from agonizing pain to emotional stress. Emotional and physical discomfort, as distinguished from concrete disabilities, are known as "pain and suffering." They are more subtle and obscure than losses of specific functions such as sight, hearing, or intellectual capacity. Nonetheless, they may provide the basis for a valid malpractice claim.

In many cases the patient is the best judge of his own injury. He alone knows the anguish of losing an eye or a limb. He is the one who has suffered from a prolonged hospitalization, or the pain caused by an unnecessary operation. But he must make a special effort to separate his emotional distress and anger at his physician from true medical mishaps, for, if he sues, an impartial jury will evaluate the extent of his injury. Problems which to him seem devastating may not win the sympathy of a group of strangers. Unless his injury is convincing, he will probably lose his suit. The two extra days of hospitalization; the additional week out of work may have enraged him. He may resent the tiny scar on his back incurred when he was carelessly dragged onto the operating table. He may feel deep anger at the abrupt, impolite manner of his physician. All of these may be serious to the victim, but are they worth the time, effort, and money that suing involves? In each of these cases, the answer is an emphatic no! No judge or jury would consider them serious enough to deserve compensation.

To analyze his own injury, the prospective plaintiff must divide his complaints into two categories: physical impairments, and pain and suffering. Physical impairments may be outwardly apparent: an amputation, loss of an eye, deafness, mental retardation, or death; or they may be internal defects only revealed by special X-ray or laboratory studies: liver failure, kidney disease, circulatory abnormalities, are among the countless possibilities. Even these, although not directly visible to a jury, are easily documented by objective evidence and corroborated by expert testimony.

Once the patient has identified and categorized his injuries, he must consider their legal implications. Because our court system compensates injuries with financial awards, one must estimate the monetary value of physical or emotional damage. In hard reality, the potential award value of an injury determines whether or not a case can be prosecuted. This may be unfair to the widow on a fixed income who could benefit immeasurably by recovering her lost $500 or $1,000 in hospital bills; or the hardworking father whose ten extra weeks out of work cost his family a devastating $2,000. Unfortunately, it often costs $5,000 to $10,000 to prosecute a malpractice case. Small errors cannot justify the expenditure of thousands of dollars in legal and medical expert fees. It is therefore essential that the claimant endeavor to translate his injury into courtroom value.

Claims of pain and suffering are more subtle and usually less rewarding than specific injuries. The trauma of a prolonged hospitalization, the agony of a painful back, the emotional drain of a long-delayed diagnosis, are injuries which are difficult for the jury to evaluate. More importantly, it must try to separate the plaintiff's true distress from his financial hopes.

This does not mean that pain and suffering never spawn a successful suit. At times these truly require and achieve restitution. The patient who suffers years of severe pain before a nerve injury is properly diagnosed and treated; the woman who must undergo four additional operations because the first was ineptly performed; the child who needs to wear a cast for an extra year as the result of a therapeutic error—all merit financial compensation. In none of these cases was there a permanent disability, but injuries occurred nonetheless. These individuals who suffered needlessly should and can be justly compensated.

However, the greatest and most predictable monetary compensation arises from clear-cut physical or psychiatric injuries. Death, paralysis, loss of sight or hearing, are physical injuries which a jury can readily appreciate. Any one of these injuries, if caused by physician negligence, can command a handsome verdict.

But how much is a leg worth to a young man? A baby's life to its new parents? Or the emotional upset of an unnecessarily prolonged disability to a schoolchild? These values cannot be looked up like used-car prices in a dealer's Blue Book. Each case demands unique consideration.

Patients, lawyers, and doctors do have some basis for rough estimates. Some guidelines are actually set by legislative statute—for example, certain states have maximum recoverable limits for the wrongful death of a child. More often, limits are suggested by precedent—what others have received for similar injuries. These legal precedents are only guides: no two cases are exactly alike; financial climates may vary from year to year; court and jury attitudes are unpredictable and constantly changing; different regions of the country view medical malpractice cases quite differently, and individual juries have their unique idiosyncrasies. These arbitrary and sometimes emotional determinants may lead to two very different awards for the same injury.

In addition to these unpredictable variables there are other determinants of amounts awarded. The court takes certain economic realities into consideration. It may seem unjust to Mary that her amputation, necessitated because of medical negligence, should bring a smaller verdict than the same injury to John Smith. Although she may be even more miserable than he without a leg, John Smith was a professional basketball player who lost his livelihood, while Mary, a schoolteacher, can continue working. The same high value would be accorded the hands of a surgeon, the fingers of a pianist, the sight of a pilot, the hearing of an opera star. Each of them suffered an occupational disability.

Occupational values are further subdivided. Thus the heart surgeon with an annual income of $150,000 would probably receive a higher award for the loss of his hand than the $15,000-per-year plumber with the same injury, although both could no longer work.

Many interesting decisions and regulations have arisen to

handle questions of value. For instance, many states consider the wrongful death of a child to have a limited value. They reason that the loss of a child causes bereavement to the family, but no financial burden to them or society. Had the child survived but suffered a permanent brain injury or blindness, the recovery would have been far greater. The permanent burden to society, the cost of his special education, and his lifelong handicap command a far greater damage value than his premature death.

Occasionally different courts reach opposite decisions in similar cases regarding injury awards. For example, pregnancies resulted after two almost identical cases of negligently performed sterilization operations. In one case it was ruled that the birth of a normal child, even if unwanted, was a blessing rather than an injury. No money was granted. In the second case the ruling was the reverse: the unwanted child, although normal, constituted a serious strain on the family and represented an injury worthy of financial compensation. Of course, had either child been born with an abnormality awards would surely have been granted, since the burden of a handicapped unwanted child would have been unequivocal.

NEGLIGENCE

Negligence, an essential ingredient in a medical malpractice case, is defined as a deviation from standard care. This will be explored more fully in a later chapter, but briefly, it implies that the doctor did something that most of his colleagues would not have done. If the error produced an injury there are grounds for a lawsuit.

Even after an injury is clearly identified, negligence must

still be established. It is not enough that an unexpected problem or complication occurred; the patient must show that the doctor, by making a mistake, caused the problem or failed to avert it. Medicine is an imperfect, complex science, and physical responses can be unpredictable. Surgical complications regularly occur; treatments frequently fail; procedures produce unavoidable side effects—all despite excellent care and the absence of negligence.

It is sometimes difficult for a patient to understand that injuries, even very serious ones, can occur despite standard care. Moreover, similar injuries may in one case be due to negligence, in another to chance. For example, a compound fracture, in which the bone protrudes through the skin, must be treated with thorough cleansing and antibiotic therapy. Even then complications can develop. If an individual acquires a major bone infection and ultimately loses his leg as result of a compound fracture, he has clearly suffered a severe injury. Whether negligence was responsible depends upon how his leg was treated. If the complication develops despite diligent cleansing and flawless administration of antibiotics, the orthopedist cannot be considered responsible. On the other hand, if the physician fails to cleanse the wound and to protect his patient with antibiotics, he is negligent and liable. These are two similar injuries—one the result of chance and nature, the other augmented by medical negligence. Negligence must, therefore, be evaluated within the context of each individual case.

If a surgeon amputates the wrong leg or leaves a sponge in the patient's abdomen, his negligence is blatant. Errors like these are so gross that any layman can recognize them. The majority of medical malpractice cases, however, raise complex issues of negligence which preclude accurate evaluation by the patients themselves. Qualified physicians who are familiar with the standard care for a given specialty and in a given community must analyze technical questions of medical management.

In the past it was difficult for plaintiffs to find experts to evaluate cases and testify at trials. This was the so-called conspiracy of silence. Medical societies still resist participation in plaintiff cases, but there have been recent changes. Many doctors recognize the need for ethical litigation, realize that patients deserve compensation for legitimate medical injuries and have broadened their concepts of responsibility to include legal as well as medical protection of the patient. Willingness to testify has been spurred particularly by the recent court acceptance of medical witnesses who come from other communities. It is far more comfortable for a physician to testify outside his immediate locality.

It is necessary to support claims of negligence with evidence. The strongest form of support is factual documentation: laboratory records, hospital and office notes, and operative reports. Alternatively, expert testimony can establish negligence. The doctor's word, supported by his experts may be pitted against the word of the plaintiff and his medical witnesses. The jury must decide which group to believe.

In considering factual evidence, a careful review of the hospital charts may indicate that drugs were given in improper dosages, that allergies were overlooked, that side effects developed without being noticed. They may reveal a surgical or anesthesia error. They may show that a specialist's recommendation was violated or that laboratory results were ignored. They may indicate that the patient's vital functions such as urine output, temperature, and blood pressure were poorly monitored. Finally, autopsy and surgical reports may uncover errors in diagnosis or previous surgical mistakes. This type of factual evidence is convincing indeed, and often it is required to prove negligence.

But such direct evidence is not always available. In two cases of negligent sterilizations the surgeon failed to perform the operation properly. This was determined only because of later hysterectomies. At that time the fallopian tubes were removed and examined directly. It was clear that the surgeon had knotted neighboring ligaments which resembled the tubes, but the tubes themselves were untouched. Since fallopian tubes occasionally reopen after they are tied, enabling pregnancy to occur, the plaintiffs carried the burden to show that the operations were faulty. Without the hysterectomies and direct evidence of a surgical error, they could not have proved negligence.

Similarly, if a patient becomes paralyzed as the result of a spinal operation, the burden of proving negligence is on his shoulders. Since such complications can arise despite meticulous surgical procedures, the injury alone does not establish negligence. There must be a clue in the operative report or a witness who saw an operative error to establish that something was done wrong.

Infections are often unavoidable postoperative complications. Therefore a patient who develops a serious infection after an abdominal operation cannot normally make a convincing case for negligence. He may be able to show that the infection was treated improperly, but he will probably not be able to prove that the surgeon caused it in the first place. He could do that only if an eyewitness testified that the doctor reused an instrument after dropping it on the floor: an unlikely possibility indeed.

In rare cases the doctrine of *res ipsa loquitur* (Latin for "the thing speaks for itself") may establish negligence without requiring expert testimony. This concept asserts that negligence is so self-evident, that the injury could not possibly have occurred without it. Plaintiff attorneys often try to introduce this premise, but in reality it rarely applies. We have seen that female sterilization procedures can fail, spinal operations lead to paralysis, postoperative infections occur —all despite standard, nonnegligent care. Only in cases such as the mistaken amputation of a leg or the sewing up of a surgical instrument inside the abdomen should the doctrine of *res ipsa loquitur* find acceptance.

Factual support based on demonstrable evidence puts the plaintiff in the best position. There are other tests of negligence, however, which can be used to win a case. Opinion and argument rather than visible facts support such claims.

An expert medical or surgical witness may feel strongly that the wrong operation was performed, that surgery was excessively delayed, that incorrect antibiotics were ordered, or that consultation with a specialist came a week too late. All of these errors rely on expert opinion to substantiate them. They pit the expertise of the plaintiff's experts against the defendant and his witnesses. Supported by his professional credibility, his academic credentials, his experience in his specialty, and relevant published articles from medical journals and texts, the expert witness must convince the jury that the defendant physician did, indeed, violate standard care. The final outcome of the trial will depend on whether the witnesses for the plaintiff or the defendant are most convincing.

It must be said that unjust verdicts frequently result,

since professional stature, ability to articulate a point of view, and even stage presence may give undue weight to the testimony of a particular expert. This problem is, of course, not unique to medical malpractice cases; it holds true for any negligence litigation which relies upon expert testimony.

Contradictory claims about the facts of a case sometimes provide the groundwork for a negligence claim. The doctor may insist that he asked the patient to return to the office the next day, and the patient may deny this. If the doctor should have made such a request, and if failure to perform daily examinations caused an injury, the disagreement is critical to the outcome of the case. Similar arguments may arise regarding drug dosages, recommendations about activity and exercise, and discussions about possible operations. The expert may be asked to base his opinion on the hypothetical argument, "Assuming that the patient is telling the truth, did the doctor deviate from usual standard care?" Such arguments could be reduced if physicians carefully recorded all instructions given to patients. Unfortunately, their written records are often scanty, and juries are left to decide whether to believe the patient or the doctor.

PROXIMATE CAUSE

Proximate cause is the third element of a medical malpractice case, and the most difficult to prove. It is the link that connects negligence to injury. Not only must the doctor have done something wrong and an injury have occurred, but the specific act of negligence must have directly produced the injury for the plaintiff to win his case. The concept is tricky and analogies may help clarify it.

A house burns down. If children were seen playing with matches nearby, they may be likely suspects. But can we say with all certainty that they started the blaze? Suppose that the oil burner were known to be faulty and had previously started a small fire. There would be a serious doubt then as to cause: the children or the broken furnace.

Another analogy can be taken from basketball. A forward is fouled while shooting and misses. Did he miss because of the foul? If his opponent grabbed both his arms, it may be evident that this contributed to the miss. But what if he lightly brushed him? Then the shot was probably destined to be off target regardless of the foul. The referee doesn't care. He is charged with calling fouls that interfere with normal play, and he doesn't have to decide whether the foul caused the shot to go awry.

In malpractice cases, on the contrary, causation is all important. The judge and jury must decide whether the negligence caused the injury. As referees they not only have to call a foul, but they must be certain that the foul caused the shot to fail.

These examples illustrate the inherent difficulty in determining clear-cut cause and effect. Medical malpractice cases require rather definite proof that the doctor caused the injury. It can't have resulted from the disease itself or from chance occurrence—it must be the direct product of negligence. A large percentage of malpractice cases fail because positive causal relationships like these are hard to prove.

It is often a shocking revelation to a plaintiff that he cannot pursue a lawsuit against a horribly negligent physician because the violation of standard care did not directly lead to an injury. Proving that it did is particularly difficult, since this need for legal certainty is at odds with medical reality. Unpredictable patient responses make medicine an inexact science, and physicians are unaccustomed to considering diagnosis and therapy in dogmatic absolutes. A doctor may hesitate to assert that his treatment with antibiotics cured his patient. Such treatments merely assist the body's normal defenses, and there is a reasonable possibility that the illness will run its course without specific therapy. Conversely, if a patient who does not receive recommended antibiotics dies from the infection, can one say that the drug would surely have saved him? It may have, but he might have died anyway.

Legal requirements do not permit the uncertainty that medical realities demand. For a successful suit, negligence must be the probable or definite cause of the injury.

Because of this conflict between medical uncertainties and the legal requirement of proximate cause, it may be hard for the plaintiff to find expert testimony to support this aspect of his case. Although medical experts are increasingly willing to point out a deviation from standard care on the part of a colleague, they hesitate to declare that that violation was a certain cause of the injury. Some courts permit a test of "probable" rather than "certain" cause, and the witness must determine his own definition of that term. One may assume that it means greater than a fifty-fifty chance, another 80 percent or more. The witness must come to grips with his feeling about a case and fit his analysis into the expected legal framework. Finding witnesses who, in good conscience, are willing and able to do that adds a substantial burden to the plaintiff.

One example of how negligence and injury might both be present but remain unconnected follows. There have been a number of eye injury cases which exemplify this "proximate cause" difficulty. In these cases ophthalmologists and emergency room personnel failed to diagnose foreign bodies deep within the injured eye. Infections and blindness resulted. Even though it was negligent to have overlooked these foreign bodies, the physicians generally won the suits. The reason: weak proximate cause. Foreign bodies so often produce a severe infection and eye loss despite early detection and treatment that even the best care might not have saved the eye. Although negligence and injury were clear, proximate cause was not provable.

Issues of proximate cause, like those of negligence, run the gamut from clear-cut causation to no relationship at all between negligence and an injury. A sponge left in the abdomen after an appendectomy is the direct cause of the second operation needed to remove it. There is no doubt that the surgeon who amputates the wrong leg has caused a serious injury. If a pathologist misreads a benign biopsy as malignant, he has clearly caused an unnecessary radical mastectomy. Proximate cause is unmuddied in the case of an individual who bleeds to death during an operation: the surgery resulted in death. (However, in this case, negligence still must be proved.)

At the other extreme, the ear, nose, and throat specialist who extracts the child's tonsils is not responsible for the leukemia which later develops, and the dermatologist who treats an elderly woman's skin condition bears no responsibility for her circulatory problem and later amputation. These are clear-cut examples. In between, proximate cause is more arguable and, as discussed, presents a stringent requirement for the plaintiff to meet.

Another and weaker test of proximate cause is worth mentioning. Occasionally an injury is so severe and negligence so evident that the plaintiff may not have to prove probable or certain cause. It may be enough to show that the doctor, through his negligence, removed even a small chance of averting the injury. A vivid example is found in a case from maritime law. Although this was not an instance of medical malpractice, the principle has been used many times in cases against physicians.

A ship's captain was told several hours after the event that a crewman had fallen overboard. He decided not to go searching for him. He later stood trial and was convicted of negligently contributing to the man's death. In defense, the captain argued that the man would probably not have been found even if a thorough search had been instituted. The ruling by the judge was based on the concept that even if there were only a 2 percent chance of saving the seaman, the ship's captain was liable for having denied him that small chance.

In a parallel medical case, an emergency room physician examined a man who was experiencing chest pain. He did not perform an electrocardiogram but advised the man to go home: nothing was wrong. That night the patient died from a heart attack. Although the cardiologist who testified for the plaintiff could not say that the man would certainly or even possibly have surived had he been hospitalized at once, he did indicate that earlier treatment would have improved his chances. The jury ruled in favor of the widow, who was the plaintiff, but the judge overturned the decision because proximate cause had not been established. The expert had not stated that proper care would have probably saved him. The appeals court, in an important decision, overturned the judge's ruling and awarded damages to the plaintiff. It concluded, as did the maritime law case, that it was suffiicient to show that the defendant had reduced the possibility of saving the man's life.

This test of proximate cause is much less stringent than "all medical probability" or "certainty." It is not applicable in every state and is generally reserved for very special instances. It is generally applied in cases of extreme negligence combined with a major injury, such as death.

This proximate cause test is commonly needed in cases involving the misdiagnosis of cancer. A physician may negligently miss the diagnosis. By the time the cancer is picked up three or four months later it has spread, and the patient's life expectancy is poor. To state that the delay of several months in diagnosis and treatment was the certain or even probable cause of the spread is impossible. One can claim, however, that the delay harmed the patient by reducing his chances for a cure, which may provide a winning argument.

In summary, whether or not the plaintiff wins his case depends upon the legal requirements of injury, negligence, and proximate cause. The chances of winning increase in proportion to the strength of each element and decrease as each gets weaker. The plaintiff must evaluate his injury: emotional, physical, or both. He must then, aided by his attorney, determine the monetary value and decide whether it justifies expensive prosecution. If so, medical experts must be consulted to analyze the complex issues of negligence and proximate cause. The jury evaluates the evidence, and if it decides that the physician's negligence was the probable cause of an injury, the plaintiff wins his case.

3

The Many Types of Negligence

J.B., a standout high school basketball player, had been suffering from a nagging pain in his right leg. At first he attributed it to the usual postgame aches, but when he began to limp noticeably, his coach insisted that he see the team physician.

A physical examination proved inconclusive, but the symptoms suggested that the problem was more serious than a routine athletic injury. His pain and tenderness centered in the midcalf, not in the commonly traumatized joints. X-ray studies confirmed the grim diagnosis: bone cancer. It was a crushing verdict for such a promising young athlete.

After the expected period of grief and depression, J.B. gradually came to terms with his condition and accepted the necessity of an amputation. He drew support from the team physician, an empathetic man, who explained that the prognosis for this type of cancer was excellent, particularly since there was no apparent spread. J.B. studied the prospects for rehabilitation and the quality of new artifical limbs. He found some comfort in the assurance that Dr. C., the orthopedic surgeon who would perform the operation, was highy respected and skillful.

Dr. C. gave him a brief preoperative examination in his office and planned the above-the-knee amputation for the following day. The surgical intern took a complete history and performed a thorough physical examination when J.B. was admitted to the hospital the evening before the surgery.

At 7:30 A.M. J.B. was wheeled to the operating room and was "under" before Dr. L., the senior orthopedic resident, arrived. He had briefly examined J.B. the night before and had hurriedly reviewed his X rays. It was his responsibility to begin the operation with the assistance of a junior resident, who had not seen J.B. until that moment.

Dr. L. scanned the X rays, which the nurse had placed on the view box. Unwittingly, she had turned the film around, so that the cancerous leg, the right one, appeared to be the left. Dr. L. failed to notice the error and did not recall the details of his examination of the previous night. He and his assistant prepared the left leg for amputation.

By the time Dr. C. arrived the left thigh gaped open, and the bone awaited the surgeon's saw. The thought that this might be the wrong leg never crossed his mind. He had, of course, examined J.B., but a busy orthopedic surgeon could easily forget which leg harbored the malignancy. However, he should have thoroughly reviewed the chart to be certain. The tissue was pulled aside, the bone exposed. The saw began gnawing through the healthy femur. J.B., who had bravely entered the operating room ready to accept a life with one leg, would now have to face a future without either.

This actual case history dramatically illustrates the first element of medical malpractice—the act of negligence. Negligence implies making a mistake that could have been avoided with better care. Without it there is no malpractice.

The shocking amputation of J.B.'s healthy leg is an extreme example. Most cases of medical negligence are far less clear-cut, and their subtleties are frequently difficult for a medically untrained person to grasp. Patients often interpret any unanticipated complication as evidence of negligence. They go to their physicians with confidence and high hopes, and when events take a surprising turn for the worse, they are certain that the doctor must be at fault. Such a conclusion is not necessarily valid. Unexpected complications regularly occur in the absence of physician negligence; infections arise, abnormalities of heart rhythm develop, blood clots spread, and drug reactions occur despite optimal medical and surgical care. What then determines whether the doctor has made a mistake?

The accepted standard of medical care as practiced in a particular geographic area provides the guidelines for a judgment of negligence. When a physician deviates from the regional standard by doing something that most of his colleagues would not have done, he is guilty of negligence.

Good medical practice, in all communities, must adhere to a number of fundamental principles. These principles, which will be examined in depth later, include the following:

Being available or having a substitute available for one's patients.

Doing everything reasonably possible to make a correct diagnosis.

Knowing when to call for specialized help.

Implementing the proper treatment once a correct diagnosis has been made.

Correctly monitoring therapy for evidence of side effects or complications.

Using due caution to prevent unnecessary accidents.

Doctors everywhere—from rural Alaska to New York City—must follow these basic principles of good medical practice. However, the characteristics of a particular area determine the manner in which the treatment is executed and the basis for reasonable community standards. A function that a general practitioner might perform in a rural area could be off limits in a highly populated city where appropriate specialists are plentiful. Two obstetrical examples highlight such geographical differences.

Mary K., a thirty-one-year-old woman, had escaped the city bustle and moved to central Alaska with her husband and three children. They found the life there more strenuous, but the slower pace and the closeness to nature provided great satisfaction. They built their modest home from scratch and lived on vegetables from their garden and game from the surrounding area. It was both a blessing and their only major concern that the nearest city with its medical facilities was two hundred miles away. The family physician was a general practitioner who made house calls by plane. He had arranged to deliver Mary's fourth child at home.

During the course of Mary's pregnancy he visited them regularly. Everything progressed smoothly. Although she was somewhat apprehensive about the home delivery, Mary felt reasonably confident and even began to look forward to the adventure. After all, she had given birth to three healthy babies without any difficulty.

The labor pains began at about 5 P.M., two days before the estimated date. Since she was familiar with labor, Mary knew when to summon the doctor and was able to reach him easily. He arrived in two hours. At first labor proceeded uneventfully. Mary was dilating nicely, and the baby appeared to be advancing well. Suddenly, without warning, she started to bleed heavily. The placenta had torn loose and had lacerated the uterine wall.

It was an unusual complication of childbirth which, if not treated promptly, could prove fatal. The doctor did his best with limited resources. He delivered the baby with forceps and quickly applied external pressure to the uterus. When this proved ineffective, he inserted surgical sponges to press directly against the bleeding site. Mary continued to bleed relentlessly and profusely. Unable to stop the hemorrhage, the doctor and her husband watched as Mary slipped into shock and died. The baby survived.

The second example is Alice C., a young career woman who lived in Manhattan with her husband and three children. Locked into the rat race of the big city, she craved a less complicated life. She and her family spent their free time in the country hiking and camping.

Alice disliked the cold complexity of modern hospitals and shuddered at the thought of having her fourth child in such a place. When a friend told her of a marvelous obstetrician who delivered babies at home, Alice's imagination was sparked. In many parts of the world, women delivered their own babies and returned immediately to work in the rice paddies. Why shouldn't she be able to have her baby at home? Alice made an appointment to see the obstetrician. He examined her in his office and explained the home delivery procedure. Both of them ignored a fact of which they were well aware: although most deliveries are uncomplicated, difficulties occasionally arise which require immediate action and hospital facilities. They derived a false sense of security from the knowledge that there were plenty of hospitals nearby.

Alice's pregnancy was uneventful, and labor began normally. Three hours after the onset of the first pains, the obstetrician arrived and prepared for the delivery. All at once a strong contraction tore the placenta away from the uterus and profuse bleeding ensued. The physician applied pressure and called for an ambulance, but by the time Alice was wheeled into the hospital emergency room, she and her baby were dead.

The two preceding stories share almost identical events, but with one major difference: in the second case, death could have been averted. In the other instance, death was unavoidable.

Mary's geographical circumstances forced her to have her baby at home. Alice, on the other hand, lived in a metropolitan area where hospitals abounded. Had she delivered in a hospital she could have been given intravenous fluids and blood when the bleeding began and could have undergone an emergency operation if other measures failed to stop the flow. In all probability she, and possibly her baby, could have been saved. It is a violation of standard care to perform home deliveries in New York City, and the obstetrician was, therefore, negligent. The Alaskan doctor, conversely, acted in accordance with the best community standards. He was not negligent.

The fundamental principles of good medical practice outlined earlier in this chapter are universal, but the ways in which they are practiced differ according to location. For instance, the physician in Alaska may be less readily available than his counterpart in New York City, but he still must maintain a certain standard of availability. It would be unacceptable for him to go on a six-week vacation without first making a serious effort to find a suitable substitute.

In the example that follows, Dr. L. was unavailable when his patient needed him. This is legally designated "abandonment," a deviation from standard medical practice.

Mrs. R. saw Dr. L. on Monday. He examined her and prescribed an antibiotic for what he diagnosed as an upper respiratory infection. She improved transiently, and then her symptoms of severe cough and high fever intensified. She called Dr. L. on Thursday and described her problem. He did not see her but prescribed a new antibiotic by phone. The following day she felt worse and tried unsuccessfully to contact Dr. L. Neither he nor his associate could be reached. By Saturday her fever had climbed to 103 degrees and she was coughing painfully. She telephoned Dr. L., who told her to be patient and give it a few more days. The next day she was critically ill, and her husband insisted that Dr. L. have her hospitalized. By the time she arrived at the hospital she had advanced pneumonia in both lungs and severe heart failure. Intensive therapy failed; she died the following day.

Dr. L. had abandoned his patient, thereby contributing to her death. He had continued to prescribe antibiotics by phone when her symptoms worsened, and he had been unavailable when she later needed him. Had he seen her promptly he could have diagnosed and treated her serious infection. By violating one of the fundamental principles of medical care—that of availability—Dr. L. had failed in his duty and was negligent.

In any geographic area good standard care requires accurate diagnosis of an illness. Obviously, the physician can be expected to use only the facilities at hand. Certain sophisticated X-ray procedures and electronic monitoring may be unavailable in a rural setting. If there is time, if special tests are strongly indicated, and if the patient can be moved, the rural physician may be expected to transfer him to the appropriate center. If not, he may legitimately dispense with some of the studies that his metropolitan counterpart would promptly order. So geographic location determines proper diagnostic procedure. The physician must fully utilize all the resources at his command.

Despite the fact that particular signs and symptoms may be common to many problems, the physician must be aware of likely diagnoses and do everything routinely possible to arrive at an accurate answer. Should an error arise from an unusual or complex diagnostic problem, it may not be negligence. On the other hand, were a diagnostic mistake to result from not making a study which most other physicians in the community would have ordered, the treating doctor might be liable.

Here are two cases in point. The family pediatrician treated a young boy for a number of months for repeated bouts of colds, coughs, and high fevers. The youngster received weekly injections of antibiotics for nearly a year. Finally the doctor ordered a chest X ray. The film revealed a coin in one of the breathing tubes. It had, without doubt, been present for the entire year, obstructing air flow to one of the lungs and causing a permanent collapse of the lung and chronic infections. The young patient required operative removal of the destroyed lobe of the lung.

The doctor's oversight occurred in a large city where X-ray facilities were readily available. It is not standard care to order an X ray after one or two episodes of respiratory infection in a child, but recurrent bouts demand such evaluation. The pediatrician had not ordered a simple test that most physicians in the community would have requested. He was, therefore, negligent.

A four-year-old boy fell out of a tree and was knocked unconscious. His family rushed him to the emergency room of the local hospital. There he regained consciousness but was somnolent and had a large swollen bruise on his forehead. During a too-cursory examination, the emergency room physician failed to notice the blood behind one ear drum and the slight inequality of the size of the child's pupils. He discharged the boy without ordering X-ray studies. He did admonish the parents to bring him back if he developed any further problems—instructions which were not explicit and meant little to the parents.

Once home, the child seemed tired and sleepy. His mother put him to bed, unaware that she should check him frequently to be sure he could be aroused. The child died in his sleep. Autopsy revealed a large skull fracture which would have been readily detected by a routine skull X ray.

The emergency room physician was judged negligent. Not only had he missed the telltale signs of brain injury, he had failed to order a readily available test—an X ray of the skull. This would have indicated the need for a neurosurgical operation, the life of the child would have been saved.

Closely related to his diagnostic responsibility is the

principle that requires a physician not undertake a treatment for which he is untrained. Local conditions obviously affect this principle. The general practitioner in Alaska can justifiably undertake more sophisticated procedures than the G.P. in New York City. However, even the Alaskan physician should call for consultation when it appears necessary if he possibly can.

For example, a young woman consulted her family physician for her prenatal care. After a normal pregnancy she went into labor, but despite continued contractions for eighteen hours the baby advanced very little. The doctor failed to recognize that the fetus was too large for the birth canal. After thirty hours of unsuccessful labor he gave the patient a drug to stimulate uterine contractions. Such a procedure was contraindicated in view of the problems with delivery, and serious fetal distress ensued. By the time an obstetrician was summoned, forty hours had passed. The specialist immediately performed a cesarean section, but it was too late. The child survived but suffered permanent brain damage.

It was within the bounds of good practice for the G.P. to perform the delivery. However, he should have called for assistance at the first sign of difficulty. When he failed to summon an obstetrician after labor became unusually prolonged, he overstepped his level of expertise. He was, in consequence, negligent and bore the responsibility for the disastrous lifelong injury to the newborn infant.

Once the diagnosis has been determined and the appropriate physician is in charge, treatment must follow generally accepted principles. There may be disagreement among physicians regarding the best type of treatment, and there may be more than one correct course of action. Therefore, as with the other principles of physician responsibility, community standards define proper treatment.

It is almost universally accepted that compound fractures (in which the bone protrudes through the skin) demand thorough cleansing and treatment with antibiotics. In a recent case, an orthopedic surgeon disregarded these principles of treatment. Following a motorcycle accident in which a young man suffered a compound fracture of the femur, the surgeon lightly cleansed the wound, sutured the laceration closed, and neglected to place the patient on appropriate antibiotics. The patient subsequently lost his leg as the result of a massive infection. By not conforming to the accepted treatment, the orthopedist had failed in his duty.

The physician's responsibility does not end after he has made a correct diagnosis and initiated the proper therapy. The treatment must be appropriately monitored. A frequent basis for medical negligence is the failure to monitor therapy properly and to safeguard against avoidable complications.

Often laymen are surprised to learn that even oxygen, so vital to life, can be hazardous to vital organ systems. Twenty-five years ago the unusually sensitive eyes of many premature infants were permanently damaged by high levels of oxygen in incubators: the association between oxygen and eye damage was unrecognized. Today that injury is unusual and inexcusable, but it still occurs. Why? Careless monitoring. Simple, readily available laboratory tests can indicate the need to continue or reduce oxygen administration.

Most therapeutic measures, especially drugs, have inherent dangers and side effects. The physician must exercise due caution to protect his patients from the hazards of pharmacological agents. A number of antibiotics, for example, can cause deafness. Many such drugs also lead to kidney damage. To make matters worse, impaired kidney function can raise blood-pressure levels dangerously and increase the risk of hearing impairment.

Most physicians who use these drugs are aware of the dangers. The manufacturer's literature warns that it is standard care to monitor kidney function closely when administering the drugs and to discontinue their use or reduce the dosage at the first hint of trouble.

R.C., a forty-year-old engineer, was rushed to the hospital with a serious case of peritonitis. His long-standing ulcer had eroded through the stomach wall, releasing caustic stomach acid into the abdomen. He underwent an immediate operation and treatment with a potent antibiotic. The choice of the drug to treat R.C.'s life-threatening infection was beyond reproach, but the surgeon monitored him poorly. Tests of kidney function were normal when R.C. entered the hospital. Two weeks of antibiotic therapy passed without a second determination. When the tests were finally repeated they revealed severe renal damage. The drug was stopped immediately. R.C.'s kidneys gradually improved, but his hearing declined until he was totally deaf. By failing to monitor R.C.'s kidney function, the surgeon was negligent.

Careful deliberation, full concentration, checking, and double-checking are essential principles of standard medical practice. Physicians and surgeons must do everything possible to safeguard against accidental errors. J.B.'s mistaken amputation exemplifies such a blunder. It was reasonable for the surgeon to have forgotten which leg contained the malignant tumor, but he was remiss in not having reread the chart and so preventing the tragic mistake.

The foregoing principles of good medical practice may

guide patients and physicians alike. Patients deserve attentive, thoughtful care—the best their community can offer—and they should know how to recognize substandard management. Anyone knows when a leg is accidentally amputated or a doctor is unavailable when needed. Diagnostic shortcomings, therapeutic errors, or improper monitoring involve more specialized issues which the patient may misinterpret. He may view reasonable complications as the result of negligence; conversely, he may fail to recognize when negligence has occurred. For an accurate evaluation he must rely upon medical and legal advisers who can analyze his case in the light of usual community standards. Nevertheless, if he is aware of these principles of good practice, an unhappy patient can begin to ask the right questions and judge the comments of his technical advisers.

Physicians, too, will benefit from a clearer understanding of medical negligence. Much of their horror of the very word "malpractice" results from incomplete and biased information. Their fears might diminish if they realized that the law does not demand that the doctor be superhuman or infallible; he must merely provide the quality of care generally offered by his local colleagues. No conscientious physician would wish to offer his patients anything less.

4

Common Pitfalls for Physicians

Disease is the common enemy that the doctor and his patient face together. Their mutual goal is to minimize danger and to maximize quality health care. All patients prefer smooth, effective medical care to complications that give rise to a lawsuit. Nevertheless, errors occur which drive the patient to the attorney's office. A physician's recognition of the predisposing causes of errors is the first step toward the successful management of disease and mistake-free patient care.

In the daily course of a busy clinical practice the doctor must of necessity take many shortcuts. Some are indispensable if the physician is to deliver medical care to a maximum number of people. A practitioner with a heavy patient load cannot perform, for example, a complete physical examination on everyone. He must delegate certain responsibilities, such as parts of history taking and drug administration, to office assistants and nurses. He must make certain decisions by telephone: a doctor neither can nor should make a house visit to every patient who calls. However, the physician is always the responsible individual—the one in charge. His experience and special training allow him to make such decisions, but he must also use good judgment. Many of the errors which physicians commonly make result from mistakes in judgment, excessive shortcuts, or unfamiliarity with the legal requirements of the doctor-patient relationship.

ERRORS IN JUDGMENT

Legally, physicians are never required to guarantee their results. The law recognizes the fact that medical realities make outcomes uncertain. One can only hope that an operation performed correctly will cure the problem, that a rhinoplasty will improve the appearance of a nose, that a particular antibiotic will reduce the infection, or that the removal of the cartilage in a knee will enhance an athlete's running ability.

Too frequently a physician will err by verbally guaranteeing an outcome. A plastic surgeon may tell a woman that the proposed face lift will take twenty years from her face. He may imply to a balding man that a hair transplantation will make him look like Robert Redford. Or a general surgeon may tell his patient that taking out her gallbladder will surely cure her pain. All of these claims represent errors in judgment, because they instill false hopes in patients. Although there may have been no medical negligence, false promises themselves are fraudulent and thus provide grounds for a suit.

Recently a surgeon treated a boy whose hand had been severely burned. He told the father that the hand would regain normal function if the scar tissue could be replaced with a skin graft. After the operation, function was slightly improved but hardly normal. There was no negligence in the surgical procedure. Its failure was an unfortunate but unavoidable result. The surgeon, however, lost a breach-of-contract suit because he had promised more than he delivered.

Another common error in judgment is to permit patients' demands to direct clinical procedures. The most familiar example involves the gross overuse of antibiotics. If patients present untreatable problems such as a cold or other type of viral infection, physicians commonly feel that they must do something. Some of this compulsion to prescribe medication arises from patients' demands: it makes a sick person feel better to receive a shot of penicillin for his cold, although it serves no useful purpose.

A five-year-old child was brought to a physician's office with a runny nose, a mild cough, and a low-grade fever. The mother, father, and physician all knew that she had a cold. The practitioner told the parents that antibiotics were really not appropriate for colds, but they insisted that he give their daughter a shot of penicillin. With little resistance he agreed to their request. Five minutes after the injection, just after the child had left the office, she had a severe allergic reaction. Her airway swelled and she was unable to breathe. The doctor frantically tried to resuscitate her, but she died.

When he was sued the physician had no defense. Of course the parents had insisted that the antibiotic be given, and they felt profoundly guilty. However, the doctor had made the medical decision.

SHORTCUTS

An efficient and productive physician must learn to take certain shortcuts. Each one, however, must be carefully appraised and recognized as a source of potential hazard. When shortcuts become routine and poorly monitored they present a significant risk to the patient and doctor. Unfortunately, unless monitoring by the physician becomes a habit, dangerous time-savers can increasingly invade his daily schedule. It may occur so gradually that he remains unaware of substantial flaws in his practice until a disaster happens.

Telephone diagnosis and recommendations constitute an area fraught with error. This practice is never safe, but a physician's busy schedule and his need for sleep do not permit him to respond in person to every call. He must discriminate between serious and trivial problems. The serious ones he must see, the others he may handle by phone. However, when making telephone decisions the doctor gambles on the assumption that his judgment is correct.

As long as decisions are carefully made and appropriate follow-up is planned for, telephone recommendations can be relatively safe. Yet the reality remains: shortcuts often become too easy, too routine, and much too dangerous.

Prescribing medications, particularly antibiotics, by phone is especially hazardous. These drugs are indicated for significant bacterial infections. Their administration implies the diagnosis of such an infection. How can one justify making such a diagnosis without seeing the patient? If the antibiotic leads to a serious reaction or if the disease progresses, the recipient of the telphone advice and prescription would have a valid claim against the doctor.

If there are risks inherent in telephone treatment of regular patients, they are magnified when the consulting physician is treating patients who are totally unknown to him. The emergency rooms of some small hospitals are covered by doctors who prescribe treatment over the phone from their homes. Since they often depend upon the nurses' descriptions of patients, these physicians are very vulnerable to making serious errors. Even if there is an emergency room doctor on hand to transmit physical findings and laboratory results, the specialist on call must beware of reaching wrong conclusions.

When a man was brought to an emergency room with chest pain, the physician on duty quickly evaluated him. He explained the case to the cardiologist on call. Because of an inaccurate description the patient did not sound terribly ill, and the cardiologist recommended that the man be sent to a hospital ten miles away, where the patient's family practitioner had admitting privileges. On the way the man died. The emergency room physician and the cardiologist shared liability. The former missed the electrocardiographic signs of cardiac damage, and the latter was negligent when he gave a telephone recommendation based upon another doctor's erroneous report.

Excessively busy practices and overcrowded offices often lead to risky shortcuts. A general practitioner saw a three-month-old girl who suffered from a persistent fever, loss of appetite, vomiting, and lethargy. He examined her briefly, wrote a one-line note, and gave her an antibiotic. The child did not improve, and the mother brought her to the office almost every day. Each time the physician administered an antibiotic, improperly switching from one to another. On a number of occasions he did not even see the infant, but just ordered an injection. Never were more than one or two words written on the chart. After two weeks the practitioner finally recognized a serious illness: meningitis. She was hospitalized and vigorously treated by a consulting pediatrician, but the result was devastating: she is permanently retarded, crippled, and spastic.

Important evidence at the malpractice trial were the office records and the office log. They indicated hasty, sloppy record keeping and emphasized a general carelessness on the part of the doctor. The fact that he had seen thirty patients in one hour demonstrated his lack of diligent evaluation. The jurors could relate personally to this inept practice, and they returned a handsome verdict in favor of the plaintiff.

The lack of careful records does not in itself establish negligence, but it points up a certain carelessness that the doctor on trial is hard pressed to deny. Moreover, incomplete records can destroy the physician's case. His word may be pitted aganist the plaintiff's, rendering the final determination a subjective evaluation on the part of the jury, when good records would have proven the doctor's contention.

A man was in an automobile accident. He was taken to an emergency room, alert but complaining of a headache. A physician saw him in the hallway, before the emergency room papers had even been filled out, and he learned that the victim of the collision had been knocked unconscious. Although the doctor informed the man that the accident had caused a concussion and that he would, consequently, require X rays and possible hospitalization, the patient refused any tests or treatment, did not sign into the emergency room, and went home. That night he died as a result of a skull fracture and hemorrhage into his brain.

The doctor and the hospital were sued and lost the case.

The ambulance company had a record of having brought the patient to the hospital, but the hospital had no record of his visit. The doctor remembered him and argued vehemently that the individual had refused tests and treatment. The jurors could not believe the doctor's contention—they were sure that the patient had somehow gotten lost in the shuffle of a busy emergency room. Had the doctor merely written a concise note he could have successfully supported his argument and would have won the case.

Shortcuts in prescription writing are another major though easily avoidable source of physician error. Common problems include careless handwriting that leads to the pharmacist's misinterpretation of the drug or the dosage, the doctor's omission of the patient's age, and careless medication instructions.

Many drug names resemble others whose actions, uses, and dosages are entirely different. A carelessly written prescription can thus invite disaster: for example, a woman was prescribed Digoxin, a type of digitalis preparation used for heart failure. Instead she was given Desoxyn, an amphetamine appetite suppressant, contraindicated in individuals with her type of heart disease. Fortunately, the woman contacted her physician because of a "jittery feeling" and the doctor checked her prescription. Disaster was averted, but the outcome could have proved fatal.

The abbreviation for "once a day," qd, can be easily mistaken for "every other day," qod, if written hastily: the difference is a major one. Also, physicians will often write, "Take as directed." If the patient believes that he was advised to take the medication every three hours instead of once a day and suffers severe consequences, the doctor is responsible for failing to specify directions in writing.

Prescription errors frequently result from misplaced or unclear decimal points. Such mistakes can be reduced if the doctor exercises care with his handwriting and if the age of the patient is specified. For example, a dosage that is fatal to a three-month-old may be appropriate for an adult. The pharmacist is more likely to recognize an error if the patient's age is recorded on the prescription.

In cases involving prescription errors the pharmacist usually shares responsibility with the physician, because he is required to be aware of dosages and the general use of various drugs. Nevertheless, a poorly written prescription produced in court will indict the doctor.

A final source of shortcut error involves subordinates. The doctor bears the responsibility for his patients, and if he delegates duties he must be sure that his subordinates are careful and capable.

When a general practitioner asked his office assistant, who had previously worked for someone else, whether she knew how to give injections, she claimed that she did. Although she was a secretary, not a nurse, he accepted her statement and put her in charge of all injections. He never supervised her to assess her capability. When one of his patients developed hepatitis, it was quickly discovered that the young lady had no understanding of sterilization techniques. The physician was responsible for the performance of his office staff, and he lost a large suit.

In that case the physician displayed carelessness by not closely supervising an untrained individual. In another case a physician was, in a sense, victimized by a nurse who undertook too much responsibility.

Mrs. K. had just recovered from a serious case of meningitis. Her family physician, as part of her outpatient therapy, was giving her weekly injections of a penicillin preparation. When Mrs. K. arrived for her next appointment the physician had left for an emergency case, and his nurse was handling the office. Since she knew how much penicillin was needed and how it was to be given, she decided to save Mrs. K. a return visit by giving the injection herself.

Unfortunately, Mrs. K. forgot to mention the small rash that had developed after the last shot. Almost as soon as the penicillin entered her arm, Mrs. K. collapsed with an allergic reaction. She was rushed to the hospital, where she was effectively resuscitated, but she required a prolonged hospitalization and was left with some weakness on her left side. She won a verdict against the doctor, because even though he had not been present, he was responsible for the mistakes of his office personnel.

A physician can also endanger himself and his patient's welfare by relying upon nursing personnel for descriptions and decision making. The following history exemplifies such an occurrence:

After her gallbladder was removed Miss C., despite her advanced age, was doing well. On the seventh postoperative day her surgeon saw her and removed the drains. He failed to examine her incision carefully. Two days later he asked the nursing staff to check on her—he was going to be out of town for a few days and wanted to discharge her during his absence. The nurse told him everything was fine, and the next day Miss C. was released from the hospital. At home the incision separated, and her abdomen opened. She required an emergency operation, suffered from a prolonged period of peritonitis, and remained in the hospital for many months. She successfully sued her surgeon for discharging her without a careful examination.

Physicians have to trust nurses and accept their observations, but they should also recognize a nurse's limitations. Before relying extensively on a nurse, a doctor should know her well and be assured of her competency. Nurses are trained to observe and to report factual findings such as temperature, blood pressure, and general appearance of the patient. Their education rarely includes an extensive knowledge of physical diagnosis.

THE LAW AND THE DOCTOR-PATIENT RELATIONSHIP

Besides poor judgment and shortcutting, a third area of physician error involves the legal definition of the doctor-patient relationshop. It is the doctor's privilege to serve the sick; this privileged trust, however, carries with it a grave responsibility for the patient's well-being, no matter how cantankerous or difficult he may be. Legal guidelines vigorously protect this responsibility.

The law regards the doctor-patient relationship as a firm bond, which can only be broken through specific and mutually acceptable means. "Once a patient, always a patient," is a slight exaggeration, but it bears important elements of truth. It is improper for a physician who is annoyed with a patient or unable to cope with a complex problem to tell him to go find someone else. If, in the interim, something should happen to that patient, the doctor may be surprised to learn that his suggestion did not relieve him of responsibility. It is his duty to contact another physician, provide the records, and deliver the patient's care into the hands of the new doctor.

There are occasional exceptions to this general rule. If, for some reason, the doctor is not able to find a replacement, he may write to the patient and let him know that after a certain period of time—one or two months—he will no longer care for him. During the transitional period he is still responsible, but thereafter his responsibility may be terminated. If, however, medica. problems arise and no other physician is available to help, the doctor may have to prove that he made a conscientious effort to find a replacement. Too often a general practitioner has recommended that his patient see a specialist only to find himself liable after the patient, having failed to follow his advice, developed a serious complication.

A general practitioner first saw Mrs. Rodriguez, an elderly woman, to perform a routine physical examination. She was a sixty-year-old immigrant who spoke and understood English imperfectly, had limited education, and no experience with modern medicine or disease. Dr. Jones made an ominous discovery: a firm breast mass and certain telltale signs of malignancy.

He tried to explain the problem to Mrs. Rodriguez and recommended that she see a gynecologist or a general surgeon. He did not suggest the name of a consultant. Mrs. Rodriguez failed to appreciate the seriousness of her problem, and it was not until almost two years later that she again consulted Dr. Jones. By now she had weight loss, vomiting, and bone pain—probably signs of cancer spread. Dr. Jones was horrified. He had never dreamed that Mrs. Rodriguez would fail to follow his advice.

When Mrs. Rodriguez died shortly thereafter, the family sued Dr. Jones. He lost the case, since he had failed in his duty to the woman. It was not enough just to recommend follow-up therapy; in addition, the language barrier, her advanced age, and her lack of sophistication added to his responsibility. He should have personally directed and ensured proper consultation with the required specialist.

Problems frequently arise because a physician fails to recognize that he has accepted and is therefore responsible for a patient. A casual phone conversation, a consultation from another physician, an emergency room evaluation, may be sufficient to establish the doctor-patient relationship. The physician may honestly be unaware that this is true. He may not even know who the patient is when he sits across from him in the courtroom.

An obstetrician delivered an apparently healthy baby who was sent home after three days. That night the child had developed respiratory distress and the mother called the obstetrician. He told her that he was not a baby doctor and suggested that she call a pediatrician. She tried unsuccessfully to contact one. When she phoned her obstetrician again to tell him of her failure, he firmly asserted that there was nothing he could do. The next day the baby died.

At the trial the obstetrician insisted that he was not the baby doctor, that he knew nothing about caring for babies, and that he had no responsibility for the infant. The court ruled otherwise: at the delivery he had established a doctor-patient relationship with the newborn child. Of course he could not have been expected to give continual pediatric care, since the field of pediatrics was outside his area of expertise, but the responsibility for the patient remained with him until a pediatrician could be found. He should have either examined the infant himself or contacted a pediatrician. The obstetrician, much to his amazement, was found guilty of malpractice.

A company employed a physician to perform routine physical examinations and laboratory studies on the employees. A chest X ray of one of the factory workers revealed some lung abnormalities which could have been due to certain dust particles in the factory's air. The physician reported the finding to his employer, the company president, but not to the employee. He was told that the matter would be taken care of and that he was not to discuss it with the patient. Believing that his responsibility was to the employer, the physician complied.

Two years later the worker developed a serious lung condition which forced him to leave work and significantly impaired his physical activity. In the course of reviewing old X rays, his personal physician uncovered the abnormal film taken two years earlier. The patient, who had never been informed of his problem, sued the physician and the factory for covering up the abnormality. In court the physician pleaded that he had only complied with his employer's instructions, but his claim was denied. According to the law, even though he was paid by the factory management, he had entered into a doctor-patient relationship with the worker and therefore had a responsibilty to deal with him honestly and completely. Management's intervention could not absolve him of his duty.

In both of the above cases, the physicians were negligent because they were unaware of their responsibilities. Those situations are unusual, but the following example illustrates a common physician error: failure to provide a medical alternative.

A middle-aged patient had gone to Dr. K. once for gastritis—a problem related to his alcoholism. Dr. K. had seen him reluctantly when the patient appeared without an appointment, and he neither hoped nor expected to hear from him again. However, he had not formally discharged the patient from his care, and he had not attempted to find another physician for him. Under the law a doctor-patient relationship existed.

Several months passed without further contact, but Dr. K. was called when the man began to bleed severely from his stomach. Although the situation was a matter of life and death, Dr. K. told him that he did not want to be involved and recommended that he go to the local emergency room. The man failed to make the correct decision of calling an ambulance. Instead, he got into his car and headed toward the hospital. On the way he collapsed and caused an accident, in which both he and the driver of the other car were seriously injured.

Because Dr. K. was legally the man's physician, he was partially to blame for the accident. Had he discharged his function properly he would have obtained a good history, determined that the man was in no condition to drive, and called the ambulance himself, thereby averting the accident. In a successful suit against Dr. K., the court held that he was the man's physician and was therefore responsible for him. The doctor was aghast—he never dreamed that one brief office visit would establish such a lasting responsibility.

Unfortunately, the routine aspects of day-to-day practice combined with the need to function quickly and efficiently make it easy to adopt dangerous and careless habits. Patient injuries and malpractice lawsuits arise from such pitfalls as errors in judgment, excessive shortcuts, and failure to recognize the legal establishment of the doctor-patient relationship. A physician can substantially reduce his chances for error by keeping these hazards in mind and exercising constant caution and regular surveillance. Legal vulnerability will be minimized and, even more importantly, patient safety and the quality of health care will benefit.

5

Informed Consent

Can a patient share in the planning of his medical or surgical care? Is he equipped to handle the complex and technical issues that determine the proper course of good medical practice? Many physicians think not, but the law disagrees. Legally, the patient must be given enough information to make a rational, informed decision regarding his medical therapy. This concept, known as *informed consent,* is firmly rooted in social and legal principles. Despite antagonism from much of the medical community, informed-consent requirements are here to stay and will become more clearly delineated in the future.

Informed consent is first defined by the contractual nature of the doctor-patient relationship. In this "fiduciary relationship," the bond between a layman and any professional adviser, there is an implied contract which protects the lay client or patient from deception. Deception, of course, can take two forms: "commission," i.e., active lying, and "omission," not giving information. This implies that the doctor must never mislead the patient either by telling him something wrong or by failing to disclose the entire story.

Informed consent has its origin in the basic precepts of American individualism and personal rights. In this country the right of each individual to be master of his own destiny is strongly protected. There are a few legal limitations to this right—for example, actively taking one's own life is banned. There are, however, very few restrictions on the patient's right to refuse therapy. Even if his refusal is tantamount to passive suicide, the patient maintains full command of his own body. No physician can treat a patient without his total agreement and cooperation.

Because of the principles of required disclosure and the individual's right to refuse treatment, the doctor must inform his patient before treating him. He must discuss the diagnosis, review the planned treatment or operation thoroughly, point out the risks of the procedure and the prospects for success or failure, outline alternative forms of therapy if any exist, and advise him of the consequences if treatment is refused. The law believes that, armed with these facts, the patient may make a rational, informed decision to accept or decline the recommended therapy.

This may sound reasonable and straightforward, but it is a battleground for physicians, attorneys, and consumer groups. Physicians recoil at the term "informed consent." They have come to think of it as a burdensome intrusion into their practices and a constant potential source of legal trouble. It is true that informed-consent requirements have become more explicitly defined in recent years, and public awareness has increased. Yet if physicians understood their legal responsibilities they would find informed consent a reasonable concept. Letting the patient know what is wrong with him, what to expect from a procedure, and what his alternatives are lays the foundations for an honest doctor-patient relationship. The law does not demand, as many physicians believe, a three-hour discourse on all of the ramifications of a particular illness and its treatment. It merely expects a reasonable degree of explanation. Most physicians would agree with such a principle and practice it as a matter of course. It makes good sense, helps the patient, and probably leads to better compliance with the recommended therapy.

A few physicians, often the most outspoken, view any requirements for informed consent as an affront to their medical authority and prerogatives. Recently, an angry plastic surgeon wrote to a medical journal complaining about the problem. When a patient asked for surgical removal of a facial mole the surgeon reluctantly gave her a lengthy explanation of the proposed procedure, mentioned the remote possibility that the mole could be malignant, and described the scar that the operation would leave. He was thoroughly annoyed at having to explain these details, feeling that his recommendation should have been enough to convince the patient of the need for surgery. The next day she called and refused the procedure. She and her husband objected to the potentially sizable scar and decided the small risk of malignancy was not worth any facial disfigurement.

The plastic surgeon decried the whole concept of informed consent and blasted his patient. He had wasted an hour of his valuable time explaining the procedure and she had had the unmitigated gall to reject it! His response, of course, demonstrated the highest degree of medical arrogance. Why shouldn't the woman decide whether or not she wanted a facial scar? The plastic surgeon was obviously unaware of or unconcerned about her right of personal autonomy. What is more, even if it were not a matter of law, it would be contrary to normal human decency to believe that he should have final, unilateral control over another person's face.

Fortunately, most physicians do not share the arrogant belief that they have the right to treat their patients as passive subjects. The few outspoken members of the medical community who subscribe to such an attitude are largely responsible for a resounding backlash from consumer organizations, which have begun to insist on impractical excesses of informed consent.

The scope of informed consent for every individual and every procedure is impossible to standardize. Every patient is different, and the amount and way that each should be informed must necessarily follow individual guidelines. A highly educated patient may want to know and be able to comprehend the smallest details of his disease process and program of treatment. A poorly educated patient might understand far less. Furthermore, some patients are better equipped emotionally to deal with descriptions of possible complications and alternative therapy than others. To some extent the physician himself can modify the impact of an unfavorable prognosis: the way he presents the information is critical. Occasionally a doctor may make a decision, preferably along with family members, to limit the scope of informed consent. If the physician can show that the patient's physical or emotional condition necessitated the withholding of information, he will find legal support for his position. The law asks merely that the patient be given a reasonable chance to decide, consistent with his ability to do so.

The most common medical arguments against informed

consent are that it will scare patients, complicate their physical problems with emotional distress, and lead to the refusal of important and medically indicated procedures. Undoubtedly these possibilities all exist, but the likelihood of such outcomes can be reduced. Full disclosure often has the opposite effect, increasing confidence in the physician.

The belief that patients will be frightened by the facts is based on a false assumption: "Patients don't really want to know." On the contrary, unknown and mysterious possibilities are always more frightening than the truth. It is shortsighted to say that the patient does not want to hear; what this often means is that the doctor does not want to make the emotional commitment of telling him. In general, withholding information is easier on the physician than it is on the patient.

There are many ways of presenting the same facts. One can tell the patient bluntly, "You could die from this operation," and hurriedly leave the room. Or, one can sit down and explain, "Any procedure has certain inherent risks and hazards. This one is relatively safe, but occasionally problems arise. Although it is very unusual, people have died from this operation, but we have no reason to suspect that you will have any difficulties."

Both approaches convey the same information. Both fulfill the legal requirement for informed consent, but one is cold and frightening while the other is reassuring. The second approach is a blessing for the patient. He knows that people die from operations and avoiding a discussion of the possibility would have encouraged his fears. A rational, factual explanation helps to diminish them.

Presented properly, the requirement of informed consent will not frighten the individual into rejecting a procedure. A careful explanation will allow him to understand the necessity of the procedure, while recognizing the possible risks. The physician must keep in mind, however, that the final decision is properly the patient's alone.

Informed consent, then, if approached with care, can be used to the fullest advantage in reassuring the patient and strengthening the doctor-patient relationship. Moreover, if something should go wrong, the patient will be far less likely to sue the doctor. If he was forewarned of a possible unfavorable outcome he will probably consider its occurrence an unavoidable complication. On the other hand, he will be more apt to assume an unanticipated problem was the result of physician negligence.

Recognizing that informed consent must be individually tailored to meet the needs of specific patients, there are certain general guidelines which a physician should consider. These suggestions, when coupled with common-sense modifications, can assist the doctor in performing his legally required duty and help with the compassionate preparation of his patients.

Certain facts add to the responsibility of the physician to get fully informed consent. The need for complete disclosure about a procedure increases in proportion to: 1) the frequency of complications; 2) the gravity of these complications; 3) the lack of urgency of the planned procedure; 4) the availability of alternative forms of therapy or significant differences of opinion among practitioners; 5) the newness of the procedure.

The greater the chances of a complication, the greater is the need to inform the patient. Certain types of prostate operations, for example, have a 15 percent chance of causing impotence. This is a high risk, and the surgeon must warn his patient accordingly. Several cases have been won by plaintiffs who became impotent because of prostate operations without having been warned of the possibility.

When a woman with five children became pregnant for the sixth time, she sued her gynecologist. The allegation: lack of informed consent regarding the possible failure of birth control pills. She was able to show that these pills had a substantial failure rate, and had she known the statistics, she would have insisted on another contraceptive method. She was able to convince the jury that she or her husband would have undergone surgical sterilization had she been informed of the uncertainty of the birth control pills.

Even rare complications may have to be explained if they are serious enough. Thus, a one-in-a-thousand chance of developing a temporary rash would logically go unmentioned, but a one-in-a-thousand chance of dying would not. The hazard of death, even if remote, is so serious that the patient has a right to know about it. The following case illustrates this point:

A young man had a birth defect involving his heart. As he grew older he developed increasing difficulty in carrying out simple activities. He needed a special X-ray study of his heart to see whether an operation could help him, and the doctor had the patient admitted. On the day of the procedure the patient was medicated, his arm scrubbed, and the cardiologist placed the tiny catheter into the arm vein, guiding it toward the heart. When it had reached the proper chamber of the heart, he injected a squirt of dye in order to take the necessary pictures. At once a blood clot was dislodged, traveled to his brain, and caused a stroke. The young man was left with a permanent and disabling weakness of his left side. When he sued, he alleged that he had not been informed of this possible complication, even though it was a well-recognized possibility. The defendant asserted that the complication was extremely rare—less than one in a thousand cases—and therefore the patient did not have to be informed. However, the argument failed, because the complication was so devastating that the jury felt that it should have been explained despite its infrequency. An additional factor was that it was not an emergency, life-saving procedure and could logically have been refused.

The above case brings to light another informed-consent principle. The more urgent a procedure is, the more loosely the legal requirement for informed consent can be interpreted. Although the notion may sound strange at first, it is only logical that a seriously ill person would be less concerned about warnings of hazards and complications, whereas they might influence the individual contemplating an elective procedure.

The most extreme example in which a court ruled informed consent unnecessary involved the seriously ill, unconscious victim of an automobile accident. Mr. J. skidded on an expressway and hit a truck head on. He was seriously injured, with bleeding into his brain and a torn segment of small intestine. The emergency room evaluation determined that he needed both a neurosurgical operation for his head injury and an abdominal exploration for the intestinal injury. He came from out of town, and no family members were present to concur with the plan. Because of the critical nature of Mr. J.'s condition, he was prepared for the operations without permission.

The procedures went well; blood was drained from under the skull, and the intestinal injury was properly repaired. Afterward Mr. J. awoke promptly and seemed to be making excellent progress. About one week later, however, he developed an abdominal complication. His intestinal repair separated and leaked into his abdominal cavity, producing peritonitis. He required a second repair of the intestinal injury. The operation was performed without incident. As a result of the complication, Mr. J. needed to spend two extra weeks in the hospital, but he was finally discharged, well on his way to total recovery.

Mr. J. sued the general surgeon who had performed the first intestinal repair. His allegation was not that the procedure had been performed negligently, for the complication can occur in the best of hands, but that he had not been informed of the possibility of breakdown when the original repair had been undertaken. That is, he claimed that he had not been given informed consent.

The jury viewed Mr. J.'s plea disfavorably. He had been in no condition to receive or understand the medical facts. Moreover, the urgency of his situation would have necessitated the operation regardless of the risks. The point is an important one: it is not sufficient to prove that informed consent was not given. The plaintiff must show, as well, that a reasonable person would have refused the procedure had he been fully appraised of the risks.

The greater the number of alternative forms of treatment available, the more rigid the informed-consent requirement. The patient must be told about the other options and must understand what his alternatives are, as well as why a particular form of therapy is being recommended. Very often a particular problem may be handled in many different ways, all of which are appropriate. The patient should not be totally swayed in a particular direction because of the bent of his physician. The doctor can offer his recommendations, but he must tell the patient that other forms of treatment might also work and would be practiced by some competent physicians.

A striking example is in the management of an ulcer. There comes a point when most physicians would agree that surgery is mandatory—after severe bleeding, perforation, or other major complications. But there are many stages between the mildest form of the disease and these severe complications which are gray areas as far as therapy is concerned. More conservative physicians might wait until no alternative remains before they recommend surgery. Others will operate much earlier, feeling that it is wise to forestall complications. This variety of possible and correct approaches increases the informed-consent responsibility. The physician suggesting an operation must carefully apprise the patient of alternate forms of therapy and let him know that another doctor might resist operating immediately. If the physician fails to carry out the informed-consent procedure and problems arise, the patient will have a strong cause of action against the surgeon who failed to provide a full and honest disclosure.

The responsibility is even greater when a new or experimental technique is going to be employed. Recently a patient was scheduled for the removal of a cataract. The standard procedure involves a surgical incision and extraction of the lens of the eye, but a new method had just been developed using sonic vibration to soften the lens. The ophthalmologist never told his patient that he was using a new technique nor did he offer the alternative of the standard surgical method. The man developed a serious complication resulting in a loss of vision in that eye. He sued the ophthalmologist for lack of informed consent. Since he was able to show that had he been told that the method was newly developed he would have opted for the standard procedure, he recovered substantial damages.

Plaintiffs have won a surprising number of informed-consent suits because of the unintelligible manner in which their physicians instructed them. For instance, several won suits when they proved that they didn't understand the word "mastectomy." They had had no idea that their breasts were going to be removed. Similar problems have arisen because of language difficulties.

A young Cuban immigrant was being treated for diabetes and a minor complication of a foot ulcer. The ulcer gradually extended, became severely infected, and an amputation was recommended. Many physicians would have waited somewhat longer, for it was not an emergency, and there was an alternative form of therapy available. The young man consented to the operation and was shocked when he awoke to find his leg missing. Because his English was poor, he had had no idea that he was consenting to an amputation. Since alternative forms of therapy were available, and since he truly did not realize what he had consented to, he won an informed-consent suit.

There are two possible legal bases for an informed-consent suit: assault and battery, and medical malpractice. In an assault and battery suit, no medical experts are required. The plaintiff must prove only that an unauthorized procedure was performed. This type of suit is generally reserved for cases in which the wrong operation was carried out or a totally unauthorized procedure was involved (such as the amputation or the mastectomies mentioned above).

More often, informed-consent cases allege medical malpractice, because a specific complication was not explained.

Prosecuting this type of case requires expert medical testimony to establish that the complication is a reasonably well recognized one and is one about which most physicians warn. (In some states, however, a plaintiff can win an informed-consent suit even if most physicians there do not routinely warn about a hazard or complication. The key is whether the jury feels that warning is necessary, rather than that it be the standard prevailing practice in the medical community.) Even if lack of informed consent can be proved, the plaintiff's burden is difficult in this type of case. As mentioned, he must be able to prove that a reasonable person, not necessarily he himself, would have refused the procedure or treatment if he had known of the risks. Such an argument is very difficult to prove, for most procedures and treatments have inherent risks that a reasonable person must be willing to accept. In other words, as long as the procedure was properly indicated and necessary, a lawsuit based on lack of informed consent alone can rarely prevail. This fact will come as a shock to most physicians, who have learned to think of the informed-consent issue as a mainstay of medical malpractice claims, constantly threatening a courtroom battle.

Informed consent is a reasonable and logical correlate of good, conscientious medical practice. Patients should be involved in the decisions that affect their own bodies. They should be told of the risks of a procedure and of alternative forms of therapy. Most physicians will concur with such a notion and will recognize that it creates good will, allays patients' fears, and is, overall, beneficial to patient care and the doctor-patient relationship.

6

Negligence Without Injury

Just as a cloudy sky does not always mean rain, physician negligence does not invariably injure the patient. In fact, although medical errors are far more common than we would like, resulting damage is unusual. Why do most victims of poor treatment emerge unharmed?

There are three factors that can protect the mistreated patient: the condition that prompts his visit to the doctor may obligingly resolve despite poor care; the doctor's mistake may be recognized quickly and effectively corrected; or plain good luck may avert a potential disaster.

The majority of people—perhaps nine out of ten patients—who consult their physician have minor, self-limited illnesses that are bound to improve with or without medical assistance. To them, the coughs, colds, aches and pains, minor sprains, viral infections, and stomach upsets are serious problems that call for the reassurance and symptomatic relief that the doctor can offer. Additionally, the doctor is able to rule out any grave illnesses that may initially masquerade as something more benign. Although the doctor is able to cure few of their complaints, he nonetheless serves a vital function: he eases the pain, reduces the distressing symptoms, and relieves anxiety. Without him, these patients might be flat on their backs, out of work, or hobbling uncomfortably about for an extended time. The experienced practitioner can usually trust his judgment that a given case is not serious, as the two following examples show.

It was 1 A.M. when Mrs. Jones finally dialed her pediatrician's home number. The weary physician, recovering from a frantic day, pried open his eyes, gradually regained consciousness, and ultimately his full faculties. Maryanne Jones, normally a perky little three-year-old, had been sick for the past two days, and her sleepless mother finally was calling for help. The physician listened attentively to the mother's description of the symptoms: a fever, cough, and nasal congestion. He asked several pertinent questions and after he had assured himself that this child was not seriously ill he offered a diagnosis—a viral head and chest cold. His advice: the standard suggestion that he had made thousands of times before for this epidemic illness—bed rest, fluids, aspirin, and some liquid decongestants. He suggested an office visit if the child got worse. As any experienced mother would have predicted, the child returned to school in two days.

As he pulled out his chair for the evening meal, Dr. Lober, a young family physician, heard the familiar sound of a ringing phone. Little Tommy had plummeted head first from the monkey bars. He was not knocked unconscious and was now imploring his mother to let him get back to his friends in the yard. After asking several questions Dr. Lober concluded that the child had a very mild injury. He would not need medical evaluation unless he later developed other symptoms. His diagnosis and recommendation were on target: by the time the doctor was off the phone the incident was forgotten forever.

As we have seen before, telephone diagnoses and treatment are often necessary; a busy physician cannot respond in person to every call. The risk involved in telephone decisions depends upon two factors: first the degree of certainty that the decision made is a correct one; second, the possible consequences if that decision is erroneous. In both of these cases, the doctors were relatively safe with their diagnoses. But if Maryanne actually had a severe pneumonia or Tommy had an unrecognized brain injury, the responsibility for serious complications would have rested with these physicians.

At times a physician may make a telephone decision that truly tempts fate. In the following example the physician took an unnecessary and alarming chance. His diagnosis, only one of several strong possibilities, might well have been wrong, and the consequences of that error could have proved disastrous.

A forty-year-old engineer, sedentary in recent years, clipped, dug, and lifted his way through an entire Saturday, immersed in his annual gardening. That night he felt the expected stiffness and aches and pains, but with a most distressing feature. The worst pain was over the left side of his chest: just, as he knew, where his heart was. After two hours of futile attempts at self-reassurance, he reached for the telephone.

His internist, generally a careful and thorough man, was particularly tired this night. When he heard the symptoms and the history, he jumped to a likely conclusion. This man probably had muscular pain. However, he felt some underlying anxiety with that diagnosis. He could not be certain that there was no cardiac problem without performing an electrocardiogram. He asked more questions about the pain—its exact nature, whether or not it radiated to the arm. Each answer gave him added confidence that this was not a heart attack. Ultimately he made a decision: he would see this man in his office the next morning.

By the next morning, though the patient's generalized stiffness remained, the pain in his left chest was gone. He canceled his appointment with the doctor and went to work.

One will never know whether this man had a minor heart attack which improved spontaneously, whether he had indigestion, which can produce similar pain, or whether he truly had a simple muscle strain. The doctor took a great chance. If the engineer had died that evening, medical negligence would have been an irrefutable contributor to that fatal result.

Patients who are actually seen by the physician may also be mismanaged. Frequently they too recover unharmed despite an incorrect diagnosis or ill-founded therapy.

Betty, a fourteen-year-old high school sophomore, left school in tears, moaning from the pain in her lower abdomen. Her mother took her temperature and brewed some tea—the universal remedy for menstrual cramps. Betty had experienced menstrual pains before, but these were different. They were more severe and in an unfamiliar place. In addition, this time she had some burning when she urinated—a distressing symptom that was new to her.

By late afternoon her mother felt that these pains had lasted for too long. She helped Betty to the car, and they began the three-mile drive to their physician's office. The waiting room was packed, but after an hour of painful waiting, Betty was finally draped in a gown with a drafty back, ready for the doctor to come into the room. He pushed her abdomen a few times and asked several questions without really waiting to hear the answers. He accepted her impression that these were "probably just period pains," and by the time she tried to tell him that these were somewhat different, his concentration was on his prescription pad. "I'll give you a prescription for Empirin with codeine, a strong pain medication that will make those menstrual cramps go away."

Betty never told him about the burning sensation, for if the hurried doctor had elicited this important fact he would surely have performed a urinalysis—a simple and routine procedure that he does right in the office. Consequently, he permitted the infection that was smoldering in Betty's bladder to persist unrecognized and untreated. Prompt treatment with appropriate antibiotics would rapidly eliminate the bacteria. Failure to treat could have serious consequences or might cause no harm at all, depending upon the extent and nature of this infection.

Fortunately, in Betty's case the infection was mild. Her own bodily defenses fought it successfully. Had it been a more severe infection, or had her infection-fighting capacity been weaker, it could have spread and caused serious damage.

Billy Walton, a ten-year-old rough-and-tumble child was in the midst of an incredible trick. He was standing on the handlebars of his bicycle while his friend was steering it rapidly down the street. As any bystander might have predicted, he fell off, landed on his head, and was momentarily rendered unconscious. In a few minutes he felt relatively well with the exception of a painful lump on his forehead and a small amount of grogginess. He balked at his mother's suggestion (they were right in front of his house and by now she was on the scene), that he go to the emergency room and have an X ray taken. His protests notwithstanding, off they went.

The physician examined him and found no abnormalities except for that painful, and now quite swollen, hematoma on his forehead. He ordered X rays of Billy's skull. Before they were completely dry the doctor flipped the films one by one onto the view box. Somewhat inexperienced, he was unaware of the fact that wet X rays are notoriously misleading. Many lines and shadows, not apparent at first, become obvious when the films dry. The X rays appeared normal, and he discharged Billy with the usual warnings to watch for signs of serious trouble.

As the films lay drying on the rack, a straight shadow, faint at first, then clearer and clearer, appeared in the forehead area. Billy had a skull fracture, but fortunately it was in a safe spot and was a smooth rather than a sudden break. It would likely heal with no untoward result. Had it been on the side of the head, in the dangerous area where one of the major arteries to the brain winds its way along the bone, Billy could have been in serious trouble.

In all of these cases the doctor took a chance or made a frank error. Because the majority of illnesses and injuries are destined to get better even without medical help these errors are frequently harmless. Although this is most fortunate for the doctor and his patient, it in no way reduces the physician's responsibility to avoid making any errors at all. Even though the chances are small that a given error will produce an injury, the more mistakes that are made, the more risks increase. Those physicians with monthly disasters and numerous lawsuits are the ones who are repeatedly careless.

The second mechanism that may keep a medical blunder

from becoming serious is its early recognition and amelioration. The likelihood that a physician can make such a correction increases with the attention and diligence with which he treats his patients. Thus a careless physician will quite likely never recognize and, therefore, never correct an earlier error, whereas a conscientious and careful practitioner will.

A general practitioner had a large practice which left him little daytime opportunity for careful deliberation about his patients' problems. He felt that his patients' needs were best served by seeing everyone who requested an appointment, but because of his personal concern he developed an excellent safety habit. At the end of each workday, often late at night, he reviewed all of the charts, paying close attention to the treatments and medications that he had prescribed. That sensible measure occasionally revealed a minor problem which was readily corrected. In this instance it prevented a disaster.

He had prescribed digitalis to an elderly woman to help her tired heart pump more efficiently. Before prescribing it he had ordered a blood potassium determination, but, during her office visit, he failed to notice the alarming result of that test: an abnormally low potassium level. When the blood potassium level is low, digitalis, a dangerous drug anyway, can become lethal. The frightened physician promptly called his patient, admonished her not to take the drug, which had just arrived from the pharmacy, and admitted her to the hospital for a thorough evaluation. Overlooking the laboratory result was a serious error, but his conscientiousness permitted a quick, effective correction.

A four-year-old child fell off a fence and landed on his outstretched right hand. He cried in pain as his wrist began to swell. An X ray revealed a small, subtle fracture line, quite difficult for a physician not trained in radiology to detect. The emergency room physician read the film as "normal" and discharged the child. Luckily, this hospital had recently instituted an excellent safety measure. All X rays that were taken in the emergency room were later read by a radiologist. If any were abnormal the radiologist examined the corresponding emergency room sheet to be certain that the finding had been properly diagnosed and treated. In this case, the safety check uncovered the mistake: the examining physician had overlooked the wrist fracture. The mother was notified at once, and the child's arm was put in a cast.

Surgeons, during the course of an operation, must always be prepared to find the unexpected and make rapid changes in thinking and surgical approach. Quite frequently a diagnosis made from the outside of a patient's body will change radically when the surgeon actually looks inside. As long as he is sufficiently clever and flexible to correct this diagnostic error, he can generally make quick modifications and properly treat his patient.

An eighteen-year-old girl developed increasing right-sided abdominal pain until she was in agonizing distress. The on-call physician and the attending surgeon examined her in the emergency room. They both diagnosed appendicitis and prepared her for emergency surgery. When the right lower quadrant incision lay gaping open, the surgeon slid two fingers into the deep hole and pulled the appendix into view. It was not swollen or inflamed—it was a normal appendix. He extended the incision farther across the abdomen and uncovered the true source of difficulty: an abscessed ovary and fallopian tube.

Thought and experience enabled this surgeon to take prompt remedial action as soon as he realized that his diagnosis of appendicitis was wrong. He found the trouble, carried out his surgical repair, and effectively discharged his obligation to his patient.

The surgeon's knife is a marvelous healer, but it can be a deadly weapon. Probing the innermost reaches of patients' bodies, surgeons practice their skill balanced on the edge of potential disaster. Often quick reactions and instant repairs must be called into action to save the patient.

A young surgeon in training had just removed the gallbladder from a fifty-year-old woman. Drains were in place in the abdominal cavity and the last suture had just been tied, completing the process of reclosing the skin. Suddenly, the anesthesiologist reported that the patient's blood pressure had fallen precipitously. Examination revealed excessive bloody drainage oozing along the course of the rubber drains that protruded from her abdomen. Her belly, flat after the operation, was now swelling noticeably. It was obvious that she was bleeding profusely from the operative site deep in her abdominal cavity, and if this were not controlled at once, she would die.

The novice surgeon quickly reopened her abdominal incision. The anesthesiologist pumped blood into her veins, and the surgical assistant cleared out the accumulated blood that obliterated the site of the surgery. When the view was sufficiently clear, the source of the bleeding was identified. A suture tied around the cut end of the artery which formerly fed the gallbladder had pulled loose; the artery was bleeding profusely. The surgeon quickly clamped the vessel, and this time tied it twice. By rapidly recognizing and correcting a surgical mishap, the surgeon averted disaster. In all probability he had made a mistake by tying the artery too loosely initially. His patient recovered uneventfully, never knowing how close she came to death.

In each of these cases the physicians quickly recognized and corrected their mistakes so their errors proved harmless. Even less careful physicians may occasionally find and repair their errors, but this may depend on chance rather than the calculated checking and questioning that is part of a careful practice. Instead of finding a mistake early in the course of therapy, the careless doctor may uncover it in the nick of time.

A family physician had been caring for Mr. Jones, a fifty-year-old man, for four or five years. He had made a diagnosis of emphysema, but had failed to recognize that Mr. Jones also was gradually developing heart failure. Although the emphysema was disabling and the physician was not abreast of recent developments in pulmonary diagnosis and therapy, he failed to recommend specialized consultation. When Mr. Jones collapsed, almost totally unable to breathe, the physician was certain that this was the inevitable end of the irreversible lung disease. He hospitalized Mr. Jones and provided some supportive gestures like oxygen, but held out no hope to the family. The next evening the physician happened to be playing cards with his friend, a cardiologist, and in the course of their conversation Mr. Jones was mentioned. The cardiologist's questions suggested the true diagnosis of heart failure, and both physicians saw Mr. Jones that night. Within minutes after the proper drugs entered his vein his labored breathing diminished, his profuse sweating decreased, and his blue color changed to healthy pink. Quite by accident a social conversation saved the patient's life.

A mistake may go unrecognized until it produces a complication or noticeable side effect. This is particularly true when the error involves the wrong drug prescription or an erroneous drug dosage. A young child had a severe throat infection which, when cultured, grew streptococcus bacteria. The correct drug—penicillin—was ordered, and the physician wrote "qid" on the blank, which means four times daily. The pharmacist misread the scribble as "qod," meaning every other day. The mother thought that this was a little strange, but she accepted the directions as written. Four days later, when the child's fever and pain persisted, she called the pediatrician. "I'm giving the drug every other day, just as the label says," she told him. The mistake was rectified in time, but it came to light only because the child failed to improve.

Frequently one physician's error is corrected by another. If the correction is timely there may be no harm done; if not, the patient may suffer.

A forty-year-old man with persistant lower abdominal pain and diarrhea was dissatisfied with the cursory evaluation given by his physician, who merely prescribed some medications without performing any studies. Three days later he saw another internist who ordered a barium enema X ray that revealed a tumor in the colon. The tumor had not spread and was easily and completely removed. The first physician made a potentially grave error, but fortunately this was corrected immediately, mostly because of the patient's personal concern and initiative.

In another case a factory employee was given yearly examinations and chest X rays as part of his employment benefits. In the fall of 1971, he had a chest X ray, but the radiologist overlooked a small spot on the right lung. One month later the man was tackled in a backyard football game and injured his ribs. He went to the local hospital, where a chest X ray was again taken. There were no fractures, but the radiologist at the hospital noticed the pulmonary problem and called the patient. The patient then consulted a competent internist and was treated effectively. Injury was averted by timely, though accidental, recognition of the error.

We have now explored two of the reasons why all victims of medical negligence are not seriously injured: they may have minor illnesses which resolve despite poor care, or the errors may be corrected in time. The third way that patients can escape the vagaries of medical negligence is plain good luck. Here are some examples of the role that chance can play.

The physician accurately diagnosed the child's cold, but instead of properly treating him with aspirin and decongestants, he gave in to the mother's persistent demands for a penicillin shot. Ten minutes after the nurse injected the unneeded and potentially dangerous antibiotic into the child's arm, he broke out in a scarlet, itching rash. Fortunately, it was his only adverse reaction, and after several hours the rash faded away.

The misuse of antibiotics has been stressed here a number of times. Generally, a penicillin shot will not cause serious harm: a minor rash like this child developed is frequently the only sign of an allergy. Occasionally, patients are not so lucky. Their allergic reactions may not stop with a skin rash, but may close the narrow breathing passages that lead to the lungs, suffocating the patient. Patients who escape the misuse of antibiotics with no complications or with a minor skin rash have uniformly been blessed with good fortune.

Byron M., a forty-three-year-old executive, was a textbook candidate for an ulcer. His frenetic pace, multimillion-dollar decisions, heavy drinking and smoking, and grueling business meetings would place him at the top of any list of ulcer-prone personalities. For the past few months his stomach had been bothering him. Belching, upper abdominal pain, and vomiting now occupied a routine place in

Byron's day. His wife, of course, begged him to see the doctor. His repetitive answer: "Don't worry, I will when I can find time."

Byron and several of his associates were at their favorite luncheon spot—an intimate, elegant Greek restaurant. Byron was on his second martini when the pain struck. At first it was mild, similar to his familiar stomach distress, but suddenly it intensified until it became excruciating. Byron clutched his abdomen, broke out in a profuse sweat, and collapsed on the floor.

By the time the ambulance arrived at the hospital, Dr. Wilkins was waiting. The bowel sounds were markedly diminished, the abdominal wall was nearly boardlike from muscle spasm. Tenderness in the upper abdomen was extreme. It was probable that an ulcer had completely eroded through the stomach or intestinal wall, spilling noxious gastric acid into the abdominal cavity. To be certain a special X-ray study would be necessary.

Dr. Wilkins knew that an upper gastrointestinal X ray, for which the patient normally swallows a thick white liquid containing barium, had to be modified. If indeed there was a hole in the upper gastrointestinal tract, the barium could escape through the perforation into the peritoneal cavity, producing serious complications or death. Hypaque, a safer contrast material, had to be used.

Dr. Wilkins filled out a request form for the X-ray procedure. Instead of speaking personally to the radiologist he entrusted these vital directions about Hypaque to the X-ray technician. The technician grabbed the forms, glanced at them cursorily, and began pushing Byron to the X-ray Department.

Somewhere along the way, the message about the possible perforation and the need for Hypaque was lost.

Byron slid onto the X-ray table and the cup of thick white liquid, complete with its strawberry flavoring and flexible straw, was placed in his hand.

The radiologist carelessly scanned the X-ray report. He read "probable ulcer." His eyes skipped by "suspected perforation."

"Take a sip of the liquid and hold it in your mouth until I tell you to swallow," he commanded for the sixth time that day, "O.K., now swallow." The barium flowed down the esophagus until it reached the stomach. As it partially filled the stomach it began flowing into the duodenum, the entrance to the small intestine.

Thus far the radiologist, peering into the T.V. monitor, was unable to identify any defects.

After a small amount of the barium, which showed up as a bold white shadow, had entered the duodenum, the doctor was horrified to see a large irregular hole in the duodenal wall come into view. Fortunately it was located toward the back, far removed from the abdominal cavity in front. This lucky posterior location saved Byron from the deadly threat posed by the barium.

Within several hours Bryon was on the operating table ready for permanent repair of his ulcer. He was out of the hospital in two weeks and back to work in five, never realizing how narrowly he had escaped being the victim of a negligent injury.

It was almost too late to save Mrs. Smith when her husband found her on the bathroom floor, long unconscious and deeply in shock. Her ulcer, unlike Byron Maler's, had penetrated her stomach lining and opened into her peritoneal cavity. Massive quantities of fluid summoned from the blood and surrounding tissues poured into her abdomen, struggling to protect the delicate abdominal tissues from the caustic stomach acid. This flood of fluid stolen from her bloodstream severely reduced her blood volume and produced shock.

The young staff surgeon at the University Hospital moved into action moments after examining Mrs. Smith lying comatose on the emergency room table. He ordered intravenous solutions and plasma to replace her lost fluids, and massive doses of antibiotics to control the infection that was already beginning to smoulder inside her injured abdominal cavity. The laboratory technician took samples of blood and urine to help assess her current status and plan her treatment. Included in these tests was a blood urea nitrogen (BUN) determination—an important index of kidney function. The test showed a normal value of ten, indicating that her kidneys were filtering efficiently.

After eight hours of expert emergency care, Mrs. Smith was sufficiently stable to tolerate an operation. It was completed swiftly, with no mishap—a monument to the skillful preoperative care of the surgical team.

Mrs. Smith would require intensive care for many days. One of the gravest threats to her life was that of infection. The raw tissues of her abdominal cavity were an ideal medium in which bacteria could grow and multiply. Prolonged, potent antibiotic therapy would be needed to save her from a life-threatening infection.

The drug that her physician chose was Kanamycin, an excellent antibiotic for the types of bacteria that endangered her, but one that presented potential dangers of its own. It frequently caused damage to the kidneys, which could be avoided with close checks of the kidney function: the BUN. The body depends upon well-working kidneys to rid itself of normal body wastes as well as foreign substances such as excess drugs; kidney dysfunction inevitably results in dangerous concentrations of a drug in the blood. These high levels might be harmless for some drugs, but for Kanamycin they could be most serious. No one knew why, but for some reason the delicate hearing mechanism was unusually sensitive to the toxic effects of this agent. Numerous victims, totally deaf following treatment with this antibiotic, are testimony to this serious hazard.

On Friday, two days after the operation, Mrs. Smith's BUN remained a normal fifteen. On Saturday the interns and residents, young doctors in training who follow the day-to-day care of hospital patients, moved to different hospital floors and patients to gain new experiences and skills. That move, normally an innocent and routine procedure, began Mrs. Smith's slide toward the brink of disaster.

The new intern was unfamiliar with Mrs. Smith's history and the details of her treatment, and he failed to monitor her renal function. Ten days elapsed before he repeated the BUN test, which is normally required every two or three days when Kanamycin is being used. Her BUN had jumped to 100, a strong indication that the drug had damaged her kidneys.

If the drug were stopped immediately her kidneys would probably return to normal. But what about her hearing? It was too early to tell, for noticeable impairment in hearing often takes from several weeks to several months to develop. Once it begins it often progresses relentlessly to total deafness. Whether or not a person becomes deaf from the drug depends upon a host of factors including the blood levels of the antibiotic, the length of time it has been given, and indefinable individual responses that make some people more sensitive than others. Many patients whose drug treatment and kidney problem exactly mirrored Mrs. Smith's are forevermore completely deaf. Mrs. Smith was more fortunate: her hearing was unaffected.

The last three cases were all threatened by dangerous lapses in medical care. They all escaped injury simply because they were lucky.

A minor illness, an eleventh-hour rescue, or a lucky roll of the dice—none of these should replace good medical care. Repeated errors due to carelessness or the pitfalls described earlier must be eliminated from medical practice. Perhaps, someday, quality control over medical practice will improve patient safety. Yet human errors will always be with us—perhaps less than they are now, but ever present. Some may find it no cause for rejoicing while others will take solace in the realization that although negligence does occur, injuries are often avoided by self-limited illnesses, timely correction of errors, and plain good luck.

7

Injury Without Negligence

"Cure the disease and kill the patient," a chilling thought spawned by the primitive medicine of Bacon's sixteenth-century England, is equally applicable to today's golden age of medical science. Risks and even threats to survival are inescapable by-products of the innovations and complexities of modern medical practice. The shining hope of each new miracle cure is tarnished by the perils that it brings. The surgeon's knife may cure the patient of his cancer; it may also bring a serious infection into his body. An antibiotic may save the life of the child with meningitis, or it may cause a fatal allergic reaction. Digitalis that assists a tired heart back into action may disturb its normal rhythm and cause a fatal collapse. An X-ray study of the blood vessels of the brain may point the way to a life-saving operation; it may also produce a stroke and lifelong paralyses. Treatments and diagnostic procedures vary greatly in their dangers, but no manipulation or medication is devoid of all hazard.

This disconcerting thought is foreign to most patients.

People's expectations have outstripped the advances and capabilities of medical science. The American public has come to think of medical technology as near-perfect. The inevitable corollary to that viewpoint is that a medical complication automatically implies a medical error. This unfounded faith in the omnipotence of modern medicine is a prime contributor to the wave of malpractice suits. To complete an understanding of medical malpratice, it is essential to realize that even well-executed medical care is replete with unavoidable risks and inevitable injuries.

Helping distraught people to differentiate an unavoidable mishap from the aftermath of medical negligence is often impossible. How much more satisfying it is for a grieving survivor or a maimed patient to heap recriminations on the doctor than to blame elusive targets like fate and chance.

This normal human reaction has been intensified by widespread suspicion about physicians and the care they render, coupled with the belief that good medicine is bound to produce good results. Just as unexpected breakdowns in a car's engine do not prove that the automobile was built improperly, a terrible medical result may reflect the unpredictability of the human body and the innate hazards of the treatment, rather than the ineptness of the medical practitioner.

The following examples explore some complications that drive distraught patients and families to attorneys' offices. In all of these cases there was no discernible medical mistake.

Harold Lindsay, a forty-year-old machinist, found that his vision was failing, making his close, exacting work more and more difficult. Finally he consulted Dr. Benton, an ophthalmologist. Dr. Benton promptly identified the cataracts that opacified the lenses of both his eyes. The only available treatment was surgical removal of the lenses.

On the day of admission Dr. Benton carefully explained to Harold, who was listening halfheartedly, about the surgical risks and the operative plan. It was his practice to do both eyes during a single hospitalization, one week apart. Some surgeons waited longer between operations, but many other renowned authorities in ophthalmology followed this practice of close-spaced surgery.

Both of the operations were performed skillfully and smoothly. By the time of the second operation the right eye had almost healed. Harold's vision in that eye, with spectacles, had returned to a near-normal 20/30. On the fourth day after the left cataract had been removed, Harold noticed that a strange, smoky curtain had obliterated the vision of the right eye. This was the first signal of a serious and dangerous complication: retinal detachment. If not promptly corrected it could lead to blindness, but even rapid action might not avert this disastrous complication.

Within minutes after Harold complained to the nurses, Dr. Benton was in his room. There was a severe retinal detachment, he found.

Without a moment's hesitation he took the next step: a quick telephone call to his associate Dr. Staimbrook, an ophthalmologist who specialized in retinal problems. He arrived promptly and began scrutinizing the depths of Harold's eyes. The right retina had pulled free from its usual attachment and was floating unrestrained in the back of the eye. It would require an extensive repair. The left retina was in better condition, but it, too, had a small tear that threatened to become more extensive. For now it could be welded back in place with a laser beam.

After six grueling hours Dr. Staimbrook finally finished. The right retina was reattached; the left, welded back in place. Although the procedures were performed expertly,

Dr. Staimbrook knew that the prognosis was guarded. The chance of recurrence was great, and each new detachment made new repairs more difficult and less promising. Eventually scarring and loss of tissue could cause irreparable damage to sight.

The ensuing five days passed slowly for Harold and his expectant physicians. On the fifth day it was obvious that the operation had failed; not only was the right retina detached once again, but the left, previously beset by a small tear, now had a large detachment as well.

Two reoperations, multiple laser procedures—all attempts to restore Harold's eyes proved futile. After six months and seven operative procedures Harold's retinas were irreparably damaged. He had only light perception in his left eye; the right eye was completely sightless.

Cataract removal, an operation so frequently performed without any mishap, had for Harold meant the end of his vision forever. He had been warned of this potential danger, but "It could never happen to me" was his normal reaction. Now, faced with a life without his precious sight, how hard it was for him to realize that this complication was unavoidable and that the doctors were not to blame.

Sally and Larry Barth were satisfied with the size of their family. They wanted permanent relief from the worry of another unwanted pregnancy, and they discussed the alternatives with their family physician. Larry could undergo a vasectomy, but his unusually low tolerance for even the slightest pain forced their joint decision. It would be Sally who would have the sterilization operation—a tubal ligation.

On Monday morning Sally entered the hospital carrying a tiny suitcase—just enough for the overnight stay. She met

Dr. Williams shortly after her arrival, and he offered a rundown of the procedure replete with the details of possible complications. She would be positioned in stirrups and would be lightly anesthetized, but not sleeping too deeply. Dr. Williams would pass a pointed instrument through the back wall of her vagina and then, peering through a special scope, would find and tie the fallopian tubes. The entire procedure should take no more than ten or fifteen minutes.

The likelihood was small that he would run into any problems, but there were many known complications—some of them quite serious. Bleeding, infection, puncturing the adjacent bowel or bladder, or even nicking the nearby aorta could occur despite meticulous care. Sally was somewhat alarmed by this list of potential disasters, but she regained her composure when Dr. Williams assured her that, although any of these complications was possible, the chance was small that any would happen to her.

No sooner had the sharp trocar punctured the vaginal wall than Dr. Williams knew he was in trouble. Sally's rectum was in an unusual anatomical position—a bit more forward then normal—and the razor-sharp instrument had made a half-inch rent through its thin wall. A small amount of fecal material began to exude into Sally's vagina.

Dr. Williams adroitly slipped several sutures through this unwanted tear and ended the operation at once. For now, Dr. Williams and Sally would have to focus their attention on this injury. Only close observation would tell whether the tear would heal uneventfully or whether leakage of the fecal material would persist. If so, Sally would require a colostomy to divert the stool to a bag on her abdominal wall, so the tear could heal.

Sally and her husband shuddered when they learned of

this imminent possibility. For several agonizing days there was no leakage, and hope mounted that the dreaded colostomy would be unnecessary. On the fourth day those hopes were shattered when a profuse gush of fecal material poured out of her vagina. Sally, who had come to the hospital emotionally prepared for a minor operation, now faced a major surgical procedure and months of misery.

For the next six months Sally learned to live with that sickening colostomy bag glued to her abdominal wall. Frequent changes of the bag, daily irrigations, occasional manual extractions of impacted waste material, became second nature though they never lost their repulsive quality.

At the end of that period the rectal tear had healed, and Sally's intestinal tract was reunited. She could again function and exist like a normal human being. For her a straightforward, seemingly simple, tubal ligation had become an emotionally draining six months of horror.

Sally was the victim of a serious surgical complication, but she was not the victim of medical negligence. Her gynecologist was conscientious and performed the procedure in the standard way. Despite meticulous technique and reasonable caution, he injured this unfortunate woman's colon —a serious but accidental complication. Even though Sally had been warned of this possibility, she found it very difficult to accept the assurance that Dr. Williams had not been negligent.

Joseph Weiner, a driving young business executive, finally surrendered to his body's demand and made an appointment with his internist. For months he had been troubled by diarrhea and abdominal cramps but kept putting off the visit to the doctor.

His internist took a careful history and performed a complete physical examination. From the outside everything appeared to be in order, but the signs and symptoms were of concern. In a man possessed by ambition and laden with anxieties these signs were particularly ominous, for they might signal the onset of a serious bowel disease like ulcerative colitis. A thorough look inside Joseph's troublesome colon would give the answer. He would be scheduled for sigmoidoscopy—a direct examination with a long metal scope—and a barium enema X-ray study.

The sigmoidoscope inched its way farther and farther into Joseph's rectum, skillfully guided by Dr. Stein, his eye riveted on the magnifying lens. Some inflammation, but no ulcers or signs of serious disease as yet. Still nothing alarming, but a bit more redness than Dr. Stein would like to see.

Now Joseph would have to suffer through another unpleasant but necessary study—the barium enema X-ray examination.

Joseph lay back on the cold table waiting anxiously for the radiologist who would watch the stream of barium as it flowed through his colon. He was slightly embarrassed when the young technician inserted the nozzle into his rectum, but he consoled himself with the thought that she must have done this hundreds of times.

The barium was annoying. It flowed into Joseph's bowel, an increasingly uncomfortable stream. The radiologist pressed and poked on his abdomen, moving the white liquid into every recess of his large intestine, filling every convolution in an attempt to identify any abnormality. Suddenly Joseph felt a severe pain. The entire procedure had been uncomfortable, but this was different. It felt like something was tearing: something was giving way. A look of fright on the radiologist's face confirmed Joseph's fear. Something terrible had happened!

It was a most unusual complication, particularly in a young man, but one which radiologists knew and feared. The pressure of the barium ruptured through the large intestine, pouring the dangerous dye and bowel contents into the peritoneal cavity. Joseph would require emergency surgery to save his life.

A rapid ambulance ride to the hospital and an immediate operation successfully rescued Joseph. Like Sally, he would require a colostomy for about six months, but his injury was more severe. Deadly bacteria and irritating barium had produced a rampant peritonitis. Massive antibiotic therapy, prolonged intravenous feedings, and close monitoring were needed.

Once the immediate crisis was over Joseph's personal misery began. The operation had saved his life, but he would have to live with this colostomy for at least six months before his intestine could be reconnected. A simple, everyday diagnostic procedure, which incidentally did not uncover any abnormality, had produced a near-fatal complication. Inconsolable, Joseph was convinced that the bag which hung from his abdominal wall was graphic evidence of medical negligence.

Louise was an adorable child; fun-loving, intelligent, a sweet three-year-old.

It was August and she was to begin nursery school in one month—an adventure she could hardly wait to begin. She needed the third and last immunizations for diphtheria, pertussis, and tetanus, commonly known as DPT, before she could go to school.

As usual, the doctor's office was a madhouse—screaming infants, youngsters running, jumping, and climbing as though the waiting room were a playground. Louise's mother wondered to herself why parents didn't control their children better.

Finally it was Louise's turn. The nurse drew the vaccine into the syringe. Louise cried out as the needle poked through her skin, but before she reached the decrescendo of the scream the needle was out.

This was a routine and almost invariably harmless injection. No one could have suspected what was to happen. Louise left the office with her mother and got into the car. They had traveled about one block when the child became agitated, clutched her throat, and gasped for air. By the time her mother realized that there was a problem, Louise had turned blue and collapsed on the front seat. The panic-stricken mother jammed the accelerator to the floor and sped back to the doctor's office. She scooped up her child into her arms and rushed to the back room. Forty-five minutes of resuscitation ended futilely. Louise was dead.

A routine injection, normally so innocent, had been for this child as deadly as a bullet through the heart. She was the one in a million children who reacts with a serious and sometimes fatal allergic response to the DPT vaccination. No tests, no known studies, could have forecast this tragic reaction.

Laura Carson was in critical condition. An infected ovary had ruptured into her abdominal cavity and caused a life-threatening peritonitis. The bacteria multiplying at an alarming rate were particularly insidious. They were sensitive to very few of the antibiotics normally available for serious infections. Chloromycetin would have to be used. Though it could be life-saving, it was a risky drug. It could irreversibly injure the bone marrow where all of the cells in the blood are manufactured. Without a functioning marrow, without those cells, the patient would die. Fortunately that complication was unusual, but so formidable that this drug was reserved for only the most serious infections: infections like Laura's.

The drug worked like magic. Within four days Laura's fever had gone down, her pulse was no longer racing, and her blood pressure was nearly normal. Each day her physicians drew blood to check for signs of antibiotic toxicity. Usually, if the drug is stopped at the first sign of anemia, the bone marrow can recover and the patient escapes serious injury. On the seventh day of drug therapy the first sign of danger appeared on the afternoon laboratory reports. The white blood cell count, normally 6,000 or so, had fallen to 3,000. The hematocrit, a measure of red blood cells, had fallen from 39 percent to 33 percent.

The Chloromycetin was immediately discontinued, but the bone marrow never regained its life-supporting function. Day by day the cells in Laura's blood fell lower and lower. Repeated blood transfusions gave her temporary support while the physicians did all in their power to restore her own blood production. After two months of a bitter struggle, Laura died: the victim of an unavoidable but disastrous drug complication.

Sarah Walker was only thirty-two weeks into her pregnancy when the pains began: a faint twinge at first, then stronger and more frequent. At first, she was certain that these were the false labor pains that her friends told her about. By the time they were one minute apart and so severe that she bent her knees up to her chest to try to get some relief, she knew that this was the real thing.

Her obstetrician met her on the labor floor and confirmed it: she was in labor. There was no way to stop this tiny premature infant from entering the world.

At two pounds four ounces, Barbara (she had already chosen a girl's name) was no bigger than a large rat. It was most unlikely that her tiny organs and poorly developed lungs would successfully support her life. Even in this age of medical miracles infants of her size rarely survived.

Dr. Hyatt was in charge of the newborn nursery. His particular specialty was neonatology: that very limited area of medicine dealing with the special problems of newborns and premature infants.

Contrary to common belief, newborn infants are not tiny adults. They have special problems, needs, and body functions that keep them in very delicate balance. Careful management by a man like Dr. Hyatt who is trained to recognize and deal with these unique people had, in recent years, markedly improved their fights to survive.

Tiny Barbara Walker teetered precariously on the narrow ledge that separates life from death. Her immature lungs struggled and strained to carry life-giving oxygen into her blood. Just as the battle appeared lost she would rally: her blood oxygen level raised by the oxygen-rich atmosphere of her isolette.

Dr. Hyatt knew that this concentrated-oxygen environment was a two-edged sword. On the one hand it was lifesaving for this child, but on the other, high concentrations of oxygen can cause serious injury, particularly to the retinas of the eyes. The end result of this damage—retrolental fibroplasia, or RLF—was total blindness.

In the early 1950s physicians anxious to save tiny premies placed them indiscriminately in 100 percent oxygen. This was before the dangers were recognized, and the result was a frightening number of sightless children. Today RLF has become rare, because careful monitoring of the infant's blood permits physicians to make moment-to-moment changes. As blood oxygen fails the incubator concentrations can be raised; as blood levels rise incubator oxygen is lowered. But despite meticulous attention some children still contract this dreaded RLF.

Oxygen was still needed to save this child's life, and under the circumstances, Dr. Hyatt did his best. He monitored the blood oxygen even more closely than before and turned it off completely as soon as Barbara could survive without it.

Dr. Hyatt's skilled treatment was to no avail. The retinal damage progressed, and Barbara faced a life of blindness. She was victimized not by medical negligence but by a modern medical miracle—oxygen therapy—which both gave her life and stole her sight.

The willing subjects of cosmetic surgery are a unique breed of patient. Those individuals who suffer the pain and expense of having their faces lifted, their noses changed, their lost hair replaced, their fat bellies and thighs surgically thinned, can be either the most rewarding patients of any medical practice or the most unbearable. Results can be dramatic, and the outward evidence bears immediate and apparent witness to the surgeon's skill.

The general surgeon is rarely praised with "Gee, how nice it is to be rid of that ugly gallbladder," or "I'm sure glad that polyp is out of my colon!" The successful plastic surgeon, however, whose skillful work visibly transforms a patient is rewarded with unending gratitude.

That is, if he is lucky and if his patient doesn't expect the impossible. The subjects of cosmetic surgery often expect too much—transformation from total baldness to a luxuriant head of hair, from a craggy sixty-five-year-old face to the smooth face of a girl, from a severely deformed nose to an aquiline work of art. Finally, they may anticipate surgery with no scars—no reminder of these man-made changes. Because these patients often consider results that fall short of their expectations as the doctor's fault, they are a uniquely suit-prone group.

Zelda Levine, a sixty-three-year-old housewife, looked despondently in the mirror. She never really cared much about her appearance before—she hadn't been to a beauty parlor since her wedding, and dingy housedresses were her usual attire. But for some reason today she felt old and worn-out, and those deep wrinkles around her eyes, mouth, and chin bore witness to those feelings.

Her closest friend had just undergone a face-lift operation. Zelda delighted in telling her how ridiculous she felt this was for a woman of her age. "What for!" she would exclaim. "Who's going to see you? Do you think you're a movie star or something?"

Her friend brushed the criticisms aside with an admonition of her own. "Just wait! You'll look in the mirror someday and hate those awful wrinkles. You'll see."

The forecast had now come true. Zelda became more and

more disgusted with her wrinkled face. Soon she wouldn't leave the house, even to go to the store, because of her mounting self-consciousness. Ridicule from her husband fell on deaf ears. Her fixation finally led her to resolve to have a face-lift operation.

As soon as the plastic surgeon saw this woman he foresaw trouble. She had placed so much hope in this procedure that she would be either dissatisfied with the inevitable scars or discontent with the remaining wrinkles. He felt certain that nothing he could do would make her happy. He tried his best to discourage her, explaining that this was not a miracle cure, but a surgical procedure entailing expense, pain, and scars. Zelda would hear nothing of this. She wanted the operation and that was that. Finally the surgeon agreed.

The operation did not produce a miraculous metamorphosis, but most of the wrinkles were gone and Zelda did look ten years younger. Nonetheless, as predicted, she was dissatisfied. The scars just below and alongside her hairline, which could be easily covered by her hair, were intolerable to her. She felt more self-conscious about those than she had about the wrinkles, for they not only were ugly but gave away the secret of her vanity. Even though she was thoroughly forewarned of these scars, which, if anything, were less apparent than usual, she was miserable and furious at the doctor. As far as she was concerned, those scars were visible reminders of his malpractice.

Understanding medical malpractice requires a fresh look at the capabilities and perils of modern medicine. Unfortunately, as medical technology reaches new levels of performance and sophistication, public belief about its powers races ahead even faster. It is true that medicine is more powerful than ever before, but inherent in all power there is danger; this is as true in medicine as it is in human society. Sophisticated procedures, complex therapy, and wonder drugs have all improved the level of medical care at the cost of increasing its complexity. With increased complexity both the chances for complications and the gravity of those complications have increased as well. The result is that many serious injuries follow on the heels of well-planned and well-executed medical and surgical care.

8

The Final Verdict

If the facts in trials could be fed into a computer and the verdict determined objectively, factual evidence and legal requirements would reign supreme. "Did the doctor make a mistake?" and "Was that mistake the direct cause of an injury?" would be the only relevant questions. The law, however, does not work by computer decisions. The final verdict in a malpractice case is handed down by a group of jurors whose human emotions, feelings, prejudices, and past experiences all influence their viewpoints. Certainly the legal requirements and facts of the case play some role in the outcome, but emotional influences may win the day for the side with the weaker case. As a rule jurors enter the case firmly committed to arrive at a just verdict, but it is humanly impossible to eliminate personal considerations.

The problem of emotional jury decisions is not unique to medical malpractice, but it has a special place there since the issues and personalities involved are so familiar to each and every juror. Other decisions that jurors are asked to make may be more foreign to them. The obscure intricacies of antitrust laws, the back-room dealings of corporate struggles, the strange interpretations of complicated contracts, are as far removed from everyday lives as the inner secrets of the Oval Office. But jurors have all had personal experiences with doctors and have developed certain attitudes which cannot be checked at the courtroom door.

These subconscious influences, sometimes subtle, sometimes flagrant, can work for or against the patient. In recent years social mistrust of physicians has tended to influence juries in favor of the plaintiff, but there are many instances when the plaintiff is victimized by jury prejudice. Who knows, the pendulum may swing back and juries may begin to sympathize with "put-upon" physicians.

Earlier chapters illustrated those principles of law that properly guide a malpractice suit. It is now time to explore some of the other factors that determine the outcome of a case.

Sarah Hayword was despondent. This was her third unwanted pregnancy. At nineteen this black high school dropout could hardly support herself and her mother with the occasional housework and laundering that she did, and now there would be another mouth to feed. She was able to give the other two up for adoption, but in this small Mississippi town the number of unwanted black babies far exceeded the number of takers. Sarah was concerned about her child. She didn't want it to grow up in a home without love or, worse, in some institution.

It was early Friday evening and Sarah had just returned from an afternoon movie with her cousin. She was the only one to whom Sarah could really talk—her mother would beat her, then break down in a violent emotional outburst if Sarah told her that she was pregnant again.

"You don't want to have another kid," offered her cousin. "Why don't you get rid of it?"

Sarah knew of some friends who had ended their own pregnancies but she had never considered this for herself. "How do I do it?"

"You just break your water bag with a coat hanger. I can help you if you want," replied her cousin.

"But isn't it dangerous and doesn't it hurt?" asked Sarah.

"Nah. Lots of kids do it. I just helped that girl who lives down the street from me. Five seconds and it was all over. Now she's not pregnant anymore."

The prospect of being "not pregnant" was appealing to Sarah. She considered the offer for a moment and then agreed.

As the cousin eased the hanger out of Sarah, blood gushed forth, followed by severe abdominal cramps. The four-week-old fetus passed effortlessly through the vaginal canal, freeing Sarah of her unwanted burden.

Nervous and slightly worn-out from this frightening ordeal, she went to bed. She slept comfortably for several hours, but at nine she awoke with a violent shaking that rocked her body. Her head reeled; she felt faint. She was burning up with a fever.

She crawled out of bed and staggered to her mother's room. She didn't dare tell her mother what she had done, so she told her that she had suddenly become sick. By then her fever had reached 103 degrees. Alarmed, her mother summoned an ambulance and went with her to the local hospital.

There was no physician on duty, but several were on call. The nurse took a brief history and recorded Sarah's temperature: it was 104 degrees. Sarah, though frightened, never volunteered any information about the abortion. Because she complained of chills and some lower abdominal cramping the nurse figured that this girl probably had gonorrhea or some other venereal infection, and she called Dr. Hotchkiss, the gynecologist. After listening to the sketchy history and a brief description of the pain Dr. Hotchkiss, not anxious to disrupt his evening with a trip to the hospital, requested that Sarah be admitted as his patient. He would see her in the morning.

Sarah couldn't know that in serious postabortion infections, time is critical; she still told no one about the coat hanger and no one asked. She was not questioned or examined by a physician. Dr. Hotchkiss ordered aspirin for her fever, but did not provide the penicillin that was acutely needed to combat the raging infection.

As the night wore on, Sarah's fever rose steadily, uncontrolled by aspirin and cold sponges. The nurses were alarmed and called Dr. Hotchkiss four times. Each time he requested that they continue the same treatment and he would see the patient in the morning. By 8 A.M. Sarah was delirious. Dr. Hotchkiss finally ordered, by phone, the long-delayed injections of penicillin.

At 10 A.M. Dr. Hotchkiss visited his dying patient. He stormed to the nurses' station.

"Why didn't you tell me she was this sick?" When faced with a disaster, doctors are no different from any other people: they protect themselves by blaming others.

"We tried, Doctor, but you just kept telling us to give her some aspirin," responded the one nurse who had been at this hospital for so long that no doctor could intimidate her.

"Well, get her ready for an emergency operation. I'll call the operating room," bellowed Dr. Hotchkiss.

Within twenty minutes Sarah lay sleeping on the operating table, a tube far into her trachea and the anesthesiologist poised over the head of the bed rhythmically squeezing the bag that forced oxygen and the general anesthetic into her lungs.

"I can't get a blood pressure," exclaimed the anesthesiologist suddenly.

The entire operating room staff worked feverishly: pounding on the chest; shooting stimulant drugs into Sarah's vein and then directly into her heart; jolting her with an electric current; trying in every way to restore a heartbeat. Their efforts were in vain. Overcome by the massive infection which had spread like a forest fire from a small spark in her womb, Sarah died.

Mrs. Hayword wailed and moaned uncontrollably when the doctor emerged from the operating room and told her the news.

"My baby! My baby! My only child dead! How did it happen? What was the matter with her?"

Dr. Hotchkiss squirmed uncomfortably, his guilt welling toward the surface. "She had a terrible infection; there just wasn't anything we could do."

"But weren't there any medicines you could have gave her? You were giving her medicines—powerful ones—weren't you?" The doctor looked nervously around. "Well, weren't you? If she was so bad, why didn't you come see her last night? Sarah and I never saw a doctor the whole night!"

"Well, I wasn't fully informed about her illness. No one told me . . . I really didn't know she was so sick, and besides . . ." the doctor stammered, anxious to get far away from this woman and her questions.

Mrs. Hayword saw and heard enough. By now it was clear even to her uneducated mind that this doctor had permitted her daughter to die.

For days she was consumed by grief and anger. What could be done? Her precious daughter was already dead.

Later that week she was talking to an attorney about some minor matters resulting from Sarah's death. She mentioned to him her feeling that the doctor had killed her daughter. He listened attentively to her story. There wasn't much to go on yet, but he would look into it. Perhaps there would be grounds for a malpractice suit.

Even to this inexperienced attorney the hospital records told the story loud and clear. The nurses saw to that. In an effort to protect themselves they repeatedly wrote in bold letters, "Doctor was called. Said do same thing and he would see her in the morning." For emphasis they had even underlined those comments.

"Once, twice, four times that doctor was called, and he still didn't get there until ten in the morning,"thought Evans.

Thumbing through a few more pages, he uncovered another suspicious finding. This girl died from a serious infection. Anybody knows that an infection like this should be treated with antibiotics. The first penicillin order was at 8 A.M.! Sarah had arrived in the emergency room before 9 P.M., yet despite ever-increasing fever and multiple telephone calls the doctor did not order any antibiotics until the morning.

Dr. Hotchkiss' violations were so flagrant that the attorney had no difficulty enlisting the aid of two well-known and highly qualified obstetricians: one from Michigan, one from Los Angeles. They would gladly serve as expert witnesses and would testify at the trial.

By late Monday afternoon on the first day of the trial the jury had been chosen. Evans was unhappy with the choice, but he knew he would be. This small, primarily white town was unlikely to provide him with a sympathetic jury. Five of the six members were white, uneducated townsfolk, born, raised and destined to die in this Mississippi community. The sixth member was black, but he was a man who had struggled hard against the odds to make it in this community. As the token black teacher at the local high school the road to his "success" had been paved with compromise and capitulation. Although Evans was concerned about this jury, he still felt an underlying confidence. After all, his case was ironclad.

Before the trial began, Evans learned Sarah's sad story. Her cousin described the coat-hanger incident, and Dr. Hotchkiss, in his deposition, acknowledged that Sarah had died from the aftermath of a septic abortion. Evans knew that this would be a sensitive issue. He would have to forget trying to enlist jury sympathy for his dead plaintiff. He would have to base his case on the facts: even though this girl contributed to her fatal injury, the doctor sat back and let her die.

Evans put his medical witnesses on the stand. They agreed that the young woman had brought this infection on herself, but they vehemently argued that this did not lessen the responsibility of the doctor who could have saved her. A doctor is not a moral judge. He must treat his patients with uniform concern and diligence regardless of how the illness developed.

The only defense was the fact that Sarah had brought this on herself. The defense attorney extracted every grim detail of the abortion act from Sarah's reluctant cousin. He kept the hesitant and mumbling witness on the stand for two hours, recounting the incident, repeating the detail, emphasizing and reemphasizing the dead girl's willing participation in the repulsive scene.

Evans and his client were at a hopeless disadvantage by

the time he began his cross-examination. He tried to recuperate some of his losses by emphasizing the misery of this unfortunate girl who, for want of an alternative, was driven to this drastic step. Finally, he attempted to separate the facts of medical negligence from the jurors' sense of malice toward this misguided girl. The doctor could have saved her, but he failed in his duty.

The cold faces of these small-town Southern jurors mirrored their inner thoughts. All of the impassioned pleas of the plaintiff attorney and his witnesses echoed futilely in the courtroom. Whether or not the jury believed that this girl could have been saved by proper medical care was impossible to tell, nor did it matter. Sarah had, as far as they were concerned, sealed her own fate: a fate that was her just reward.

It took just thirty minutes for the jury to return the verdict: "Not guilty."

Dr. Hotchkiss had been negligent. His negligence was the proximate cause of Sarah's death, for if he had seen and treated her twelve hours earlier she would almost surely have survived. The injury is apparent since Sarah died. Thus all of the required components for a valid malpractice suit —negligence, proximate cause, and injury were vividly and unquestionably present. This was a meritorious plaintiff case that failed to sway a biased jury.

Here is another case where emotion, not justice, triumphed. It had become almost a ritual that summer. After a long day of sunning beside the baby pool, Miriam Greene would drive three-year-old David home, bathe him, dress him in his shortie pajamas imprinted with poses of a daredevil on his motorcycle, and prepare dinner while he rode his tricycle around the patio. David was tall for his age, and it made Miriam proud when, because of both his size and his mature vocabulary, people mistook him for four or five years old. Actually, his size was also something of a minor problem. He seemed to outgrow his clothing "before the dirt of the first wearing was washed out," so Steven, his adoring father, was fond of saying. These particular pajamas, Miriam smiled to herself, had been the source of repeated battles: too tight, torn, missing one button, undoubtedly ready for retirement, but David had refused to sleep without them for the last month.

Dinner was the usual happy babble of conversation—Steven recounting his day, David describing the morning's *Sesame Street* program—that ended abruptly at the ring of a bell—the ice-cream truck making its evening rounds.

Father and son headed down the driveway for the truck. To avoid blocking traffic the driver always parked his truck at the far edge of the cul-de-sac, but an impatient motorist collided violently with David, as the child bolted into the street.

Steven lifted his son off the road. David wasn't bleeding, but the boy was unconscious and limp in his arms. He gently laid the boy flat on the pavement, trying not to move his head from side to side, told the gathering crowd to keep back. As he looked up past Miriam's tear-streaked face, he saw the ambulance pulling up.

David awoke in the ambulance, confused at first and then crying when his bruised right leg began to throb. But by the time they arrived at the emergency room David was totally immersed in the excitement of the siren and the flashing lights, and Steven was beginning to hope that his son might not be seriously injured.

Bustling nurses and physicians, X-ray technicians, the consultant radiologist and all of their tests, pictures, and examinations seemed almost anticlimatic, Steven mused. He and Miriam felt more relaxed and reassured each moment as David launched into his full-blown performance for appreciative adults: counting from one to twenty first in English, then in Spanish, the recitation of his name, telephone number, and address, and at least twelve Mother Goose rhymes.

When the consultant neurosurgeon said that all the tests were negative, Steven was hardly surprised. Miriam was given the standard "head sheet" that listed dangerous signs —headache, vomiting, extreme drowsiness—that should prompt an immediate return to the hospital. As they lifted him from the examining table, David was regaling the assembled adults with tales about Evel Knievel's motorcycle exploits as depicted on his slightly torn but otherwise unharmed pajamas.

They managed to keep David down for almost three days, but then David and Steven were again part of the clamoring crowd that surrounded the ice-cream truck. Miriam began loading the dishwasher as David sat on the porch licking his popsicle. She heard David's mild complaint that "the inside hurt" as he swallowed, and she made a mental note to check his throat before bed. However, his complaints became more insistent and he put down the popsicle. Steven looked alarmed, but practical Miriam moved David to the lighted corner of the porch, had him open his mouth, and was confronted by a tongue completely reddened by the partially eaten popsicle. It would be futile to look for an inflamed throat now.

Suddenly David coughed, and Miriam jumped involuntarily as what appeared to be a small piece of red ice flew toward her shoulder. Steven screamed, "Miriam, it's blood!"

David moaned in pain, then choked. His parents were transfixed with horror as they watched the stream of bright red blood pour from his mouth and cover his body and the floor. The blood continued to gush until the child's body became limp. David was dead.

After numb shock ended, they demanded to know how this was possible and why it was not predicted by the physicians who saw David after the accident. The autopsy gave only partial answers: a tear, no doubt caused by the accident but initially small, had occurred in the aorta, the body's largest artery which carries blood directly from the heart. Blood continually pounding against the esophagus which lies just in front of it had eroded through this soft-walled tube which connects the mouth to the stomach. The unrelenting pressure of the blood pulsing through the aorta extended the tear in the esophagus. David had bled to death as his blood raced from the aorta through the tear and out of his mouth.

Their family physician vainly explained to Miriam and Steven that this type of injury is rare, virtually undetectable until specific symptoms appear, and untreatable once the bleeding begins so suddenly and so vigorously.

Bitter and inconsolable, Miriam and Steven felt that someone among the physicians who attended David the first night in the emergency room should have at least suspected the possibility of this kind of injury. Yet no one had cautioned them about anything but the symptoms of a brain contusion;

no one had given them any warning—nothing but reassurance.

Vengeance and retribution became the passions that consumed Miriam's waking moments. When Steven nearly became convinced by their lawyer that there were no grounds for a malpractice suit, Miriam insisted that he seek another opinion and then a third, until they found someone who was willing to pursue the case in court.

Jeb Pearson was young and ambitious. His driving single-mindedness was hardly an endearing personality trait. He felt, with some justification, rejected by his peers, but he took consolation in the belief that he would be more successful than any of them.

His inexperience with medical malpractice work did not disturb him. Pearson had long ago determined that the only cure for inexperience was experience, which was never obtained unless one took chances. But for him taking chances never meant being foolhardy. He invariably started with the deck stacked in his favor even when the case, on the surface, appeared hopeless.

The Greenes had brought with them the expert medical opinion obtained by the first attorney. Pearson read it over and over, hoping to find something questionable, something equivocal, something arguable. He could find nothing that would support his case. Undaunted, he submitted the medical records first to one, then to a second medical expert. Both concurred with the original opinion: David's death was tragic but unavoidable.

Although Pearson believed the experts, he shrewdly recognized that the horrible circumstances of David's death before the eyes of his helpless parents, coupled with their still obvious grief, would provide unbeatable jury appeal. He knew that it would be impossible to get a medical expert to testify that David's physicians had been negligent, so he decided to use another rule of law to get the case to trial without expert testimony. He would try to introduce the doctrine of *res ipsa loquitur*, which argued that the facts spoke for themselves and eliminated the need for a medical expert.

After all, the facts did speak for themselves: David Greene was seen in the emergency room by several physicians and three days later he was dead. Pearson realized that he'd have to do a lot of fast talking to get that by a judge, but he'd done that before. That was the hardest part of this case; once he faced a jury he would be at his best, orchestrating their responses to the emotional appeal he'd planned.

Judge Holt heard the defense attorney speak first, asking for a summary judgment and dismissal before the case went to trial because there were no grounds for a suit and no expert witnesses to testify. The judge would hear Mr. Pearson's counter argument before rendering a decision.

The defense attorney rightly protested that *res ipsa loquitur* could not be applied in this case since, Mr. Pearson's flamboyant protests to the contrary, negligence did not exist. But the judge was impressed by Pearson's mellow voice and erudite presentation. The defense attorney objected in vain to the lapses in logic and law that pervaded Pearson's convoluted arguments; Judge Holt was caught in the web Pearson was spinning. The argument for *res ipsa loquitur* had never, he felt, been so cleverly argued although some of it, to be sure, was a bit abstruse. Judge Holt rewarded the masterful oration with a jury trial.

The trial itself was formulated in Pearson's mind as a playwright plans a play; not only the words, but the gestures, the costumes, the movements, and even the props, each timed to exert the maximum effect on the audience—the jury.

As always, the plaintiff's case would be presented first. The strength of his appeal would have to be so strong that it would make the jury impervious to any testimony that followed. The defense testimony—the recitation of events in the emergency room, the disclaimers of negligence—would have to be accepted without rebuttal. But Pearson hoped that by the time the defense took the stand the case would be over.

Steven was sworn in first. Guided by Pearson, he recounted the events of the accident, the ride to the hospital, David's recovery, and even, with Pearson's careful manipulations, David's rhyme recitation and his entertaining of the emergency room crew by counting in Spanish. Steven remained composed, faltering only when describing David's attire—his motorcycle pajamas.

Steven was just a preliminary to Miriam—the childless, sorrowful mother. Softly Pearson began the questioning, careful to stay in safe territory, holding her trembling emotions in check. He was even able to get Miriam to smile as she related her happiness at David's apparent recovery after the accident.

Then Pearson started questioning her about the boy's death. Miriam started to relive the last night: David's cough, that gurgle of death as he collapsed before their eyes. She had to stop momentarily, and Pearson, walking to the plaintiff's table, sipped a glass of water and unobtrusively slipped something from his briefcase.

Recomposed, Miriam looked up just as Pearson reached the witness box. "Would you identify this article of clothing?" he asked.

The jury gasped and Miriam screamed as Pearson held the two pieces of David's bloodied motorcycle pajamas for everyone to see.

In the numbed shock that followed, the objections of the defense and the rebukes of the judge were wasted. No court admonition to "disregard that piece of evidence" could ever strike the image of those pajamas from the mind of every juror.

The arguments of the defense attorney and the medical truths offered by the defense witnesses in the next days rang futilely through the courtroom. It took the jury fifteen minutes to award the grieving parents $250,000.

Negligence, proximate cause, and injury are the principles set forth in the law to bring some order to the judicial processes. Those accounts of bias, emotionalism, and trickery bear witness to the twists and perversions of that order.

In the next chapter the reader should follow the case thoughtfully from the initial injury to the conclusion of the jury debate, always mindful of the legal requirements—negligence, proximate cause, and injury. He must try to abstract himself from the emotionalism of the case in an effort to arrive at his own just verdict. Separated from the excitement and appeal of the courtroom setting, he can compare his conclusion with the final decision rendered by the jury.

9

From Hospital Bed to Jury Decision

Part I—The Injury

The car moved slowly down the San Antonio boulevard. It was 8 P.M. and the visibility was almost obscured by the drizzling rain. Leon Klineberg, a prominent architect, had just completed an unusually busy week. They were all hectic, but this was worse than most. He looked forward with great anticipation to two days of rest, an anticipation heightened by the arrival of his daughter and grandchildren from California.

He reached the intersection of Pasteur and Mayo Drives. Despite the fact that the community had petitioned for stoplights here, the only traffic controls were partially obscured four-way stop signs. Leon stopped, looked around, then crept forward. His vision was blocked by a parked car and the heavy foliage, and he was unaware of the motorist approaching at breakneck speed. When Leon's car pulled slowly out it was too late to avoid a collision. Brakes screeched, and Leon momentarily sensed the violent impact which hurled him across the front seat of his car.

His reckless teen-aged assailant was shaken but not seriously injured. He found Leon stretched unconscious across the front seat. Within moments the highway patrol arrived, followed shortly by the Fire Rescue Squad. The attendants carefully lifted Leon through the rear door of the ambulance and sped to the County Hospital.

By the time he reached the emergency room Leon had regained consciousness, although he was still confused and groggy. Dr. Little, a surgical resident, inquired about specific symptoms—the first step in identifying Leon's injuries.

"All I know is my head and neck hurt like hell."

Next the physical examination: starting from the head and working down Leon's body, Dr. Little scrutinized his pupils, the insides of his eyes, his scalp and face. He listened carefully to his heart and lungs, then manually indented every recess of Leon's middle-aged abdominal spread. Thus far there was no cause for alarm.

The critically important neurological examination, generally reserved for last, began.

"Lift up your legs, Mr. Klineberg."

No response.

"Can you move your legs?"

Leon concentrated. That simple function no longer responded to his brain's command.

"How about your arms?"

Not even a flicker of motion. Dr. Little pulled a pin from his black bag.

"Can you feel this?"

Leon felt the pain in his legs, but his arms were nearly devoid of sensation.

Paralysis? The vague impression Leon was gleaning from the doctor's examination suddenly blazed into focus: he was paralyzed!

"What's wrong with me? I can't move!" Leon cried.

The neck pain and paralysis meant one thing: a severe disruption of the spinal cord as it passed from the brain through the neck. The young sandy-haired physician spoke reassuringly—as reassuringly as humanly possible to a man acutely paralyzed.

"It looks like you have a spinal injury. I can't tell how serious it is yet, but I'll get some X rays and ask Dr. Stanton, the neurosurgeon, to come in. I don't want you to move your head."

Dr. Little supported Leon's head with sandbags and admonished the nursing personnel to avoid moving it. He knew that with one wrong turn a fractured bone could slash through the spinal cord like a knife, causing permanent paralysis or even immediate death.

By the time the X rays were dry Dr. Stanton was on the scene. The films showed no injury to the spinal column itself—no fracture or dislocation. It was one of those mysterious spinal cord injuries—perhaps produced by a transient dislocation of the spine, a ruptured disk, or some other crushing force delivered to the cord.

Dr. Stanton introduced himself to Leon, then began a thorough neurological examination. Good documentation from the start would permit an accurate assessment of day-to-day changes and progress. Dr. Stanton tested each muscle group individually, eliciting reflexes with his hammer and recording all aspects of sensory function—light touch, pain sensation, vibratory appreciation, and position sense. Each of these unique functions had a special place in the spinal nerve network. Each meant something specific to the trained neurosurgeon, telling him the extent and severity of the cord injury.

Leon had only minimal preservation of motor function. He could move his right leg ever so slightly, hardly more than a flicker. The fingers of his right hand offered the faintest sign of life. His left arm and leg, paralyzed more severely, lay motionless. He retained most of the sensation in his legs, but his arms had little feeling at all. As is often true in patients with these injuries, Leon had no voluntary control over his bladder or bowel function—an intolerable situation for this particularly fastidious man.

Dr. Stanton cautiously inserted a needle into the lower part of his spinal canal to measure the pressure of the spinal fluid. This would help to delineate the severity of the cord injury and, more importantly, tell whether an emergency operation might be required. A complete block of the spinal fluid as it reached the area of the neck injury would be ominous. A partial block, or no block at all, would recommend against immediate surgery. Dr. Stanton attached a long, stiff plastic tube to the spinal needle, and filled it with a salt solution. The column of liquid rose slowly then fell. Pressure on Leon's neck against the jugular vein caused a slow but distinct jump in the fluid column. There was evidence of some obstruction of the spinal canal, but it was incomplete—an emergency operation would not be necessary.

Dr. Stanton supervised the attendants as they lifted Leon onto a special bed designed for patients with spinal cord injuries. Fifteen-pound weights dangled from the end of the bed, attached via a pulley and rope to Leon's head. In the absence of a dislocation, traction would not be likely to help, but it was harmless and worth a try. The nurses, instructed by Dr. Stanton's handwritten orders, began their round-the-clock vigil.

Now Leon sought answers to the terrifying questions filling his mind.

How serious was the injury? Would he walk again? What did the X rays show? What would Dr. Stanton do next?

Dr. Stanton sympathetically but frankly revealed the gravity of the injury. He indicated that the prognosis was quite variable from case to case and was always uncertain immediately after such an injury. A period of watchful and hopeful anticipation was the only possible course of action. Leon might never walk or use his arms again, or his paralysis might be temporary. The outcome would depend upon the extent of permanent injury to the delicate cord tissue—a secret that only time would reveal.

The first few days brought encouraging signs. Leon could move his right leg higher than before and could now bend his right elbow. By the fifth day he could slide his right arm along his chest to his mouth and hold his own cigarette if it were placed between his motionless fingers. Still, a severely disabling degree of paralysis remained.

Leon's family provided the strong emotional support so essential to his continued perseverance. His wife was with him day and night. His daughter spent every possible moment by his bedside. His nineteen-year-old son returned from college to offer his assistance and comfort to his stricken father.

Each new flicker of motor activity, each bit of added strength brought joy and hope to the hearts of Leon, his family, and the nurses who constantly attended him. Now he could wiggle a few of his toes, now added flexion of the right knee, now he could almost reach his chest with his knee. Gravity, a vague memory from high school physics, was his daily adversary. At one point his son placed several fishing sinkers on Leon's fingers to check his strength. Leon could raise them above the bed haltingly one by one.

"C'mon, Dad," his son encouraged, "you can lift them higher."

Leon tried, but his fingers wouldn't follow his most forceful commands and deepest concentration. Each day for a week this scene was repeated.

"C'mon, just a little higher."

Every millimeter of new movement, real or conjured from his bones, delighted Leon's persistent son.

"I'm sure you're getting better. I know you can move those fingers much higher than you could when I first saw you."

Dr. Stanton conducted his own examinations. At first he, too, was hopeful, but hope changed to uncertainty and then to despair as the progress slowed to an imperceptible crawl. While Leon was certain that he would soon be running with his grandchildren, Dr. Stanton foresaw an invalid's life. After seventeen days of little change Dr. Stanton presented his dire thoughts to the Klineberg family.

He explained that although there had been some minor improvement, Leon had reached a plateau. There were, at this point, two alternative courses of action. Either they proceed in the same way with physical therapy and hopeful anticipation, or they could perform a myelogram—a special X ray of the spinal canal—to determine whether or not an operation might be of benefit. With or without the operation, the chances for recovery were very small indeed. There was unanimous agreement: perform the X-ray study.

The dye injected into Leon's spinal canal by the radiologist flowed downward toward his head, as he lay upside down on the special table. When it reached the neck it stopped momentarily, then slowly inched its way by a partial obstruction. This was the site of the trouble. Whether this block was due to swelling of the spinal cord itself, to a collection of blood outside the cord, or to a ruptured disk was something this study could not determine. The X ray was consistent with any one, or all three, of these possibilities.

Now came the decision: to operate or not. This was one of those many highly controversial gray areas of medicine. Many neurosurgeons feel that surgery is never appropriate for this condition. Others argue vehemently that it is mandatory. Most agree either approach is reasonable and proper.

Dr. Stanton recommended the operation, but the final decision was Leon's. He explained that relieving some of the pressure on the spinal cord might prevent further damage to any nerve cells that had survived the destruction of the crushing injury. The operation offered little hope for success, but so did inaction. At least if he operated, Dr. Stanton and Leon would feel that they had done everything in their power to reverse his otherwise inevitable life of immobility. The physician cautioned, however, that the operation could cause additional injury and retard additional progress or destroy what little function had already returned.

Leon wanted to give himself every possible chance. How devastating to remain paralyzed, always wondering whether an operation might have produced a miraculous improvement. By now he realized that his progress, despite the optimistic observations by his family, was minimal at best.

Accepting the fact that inaction would almost surely end in total and permanent paralysis, Leon agreed to the surgery.

The knife glided smoothly through the skin on the back of Leon's neck as the laminectomy began. As Dr. Stanton carefully separated the muscles overlying the vertebral bodies—those bones in the neck that support the head and protect the vulnerable spinal cord—he wondered what awaited him inside. Would there be a protruding disk? Would the cord be massively swollen? Would there be a large blood clot in the depths of the spinal tissue itself?

The saw cut through the bone, then the rongeurs, a crushing device, gnawed away at the remaining fragments that blocked access to the spinal canal. As the spinal cord came into view, Dr. Stanton's hopes fell. The cord was not greatly swollen and there was no protrusion of disk material. There was less pressure on the spinal cord than Dr. Stanton had expected, and it was unlikely that the operation would do much good.

"Mr. Klineberg," he thought, "the inside of your spinal cord must be badly damaged."

For several days after the operation Leon lay motionless, unable or unwilling to move because of the agonizing pain in his neck. Much of the stoicism and self-confidence of earlier days in the hospital had vanished. When he finally tried to move he was barely able to exact a flicker of response from his limbs. The function in his right side, which seemed promising before the operation, was nearly gone.

It was too early to tell whether this worsening was temporary or permanent. Swelling and pain from the operation could cause a short-lived deterioration. Operative dissection and interference with the blood supply to the spinal cord could also have produced more serious, permanent damage to those delicate nerves, as Dr. Stanton had warned.

Leon was enveloped by despair. This last-ditch effort, the operation, had failed. Grief-stricken, Leon surrendered. He refused to play the weight-on-the-fingers game with his son. He would never discover what function could be recovered through continued determination.

Recriminations started to boil up as Leon and his family faced this devastating and now, surely, permanent injury. First they centered on the teen-ager whose recklessness robbed Leon of his healthy body, then on the abrupt change following the operation. They began to wonder.

"Was Dr. Stanton right? Should he have operated? Was the operation performed correctly?"

As these questions became more frequent, their belief that Dr. Stanton had made an error increased. Shortly after Leon was sent to a rehabilitation hospital, where they would make the most of what little movement remained, his wife contacted a local attorney about a possible lawsuit.

Mrs. Klineberg was referred by her family's personal attorney to Andrew Carter, a dynamic, experienced negligence lawyer. He had successfully tried many malpractice cases, and on a number of occasions had won enormous verdicts.

Carter was unfamiliar with neurosurgery and this type of injury, but the damage value, potentially staggering, was well worth the time and expense of a preliminary investigation. After all, this fifty-year-old architect was a senior partner in one of the largest firms in the country. His lost income alone would be worth three million dollars, not to mention the immeasurable value of the pain and suffering of lifelong paralysis.

Carter had an extensive medical library, including several major textbooks in neurosurgery. Each of them emphasized the widespread controversy surrounding Leon's type of injury and its treatment. Since a physician's action must be judged by the standards of his community, such a controversy weakens a plaintiff claim. Had Carter consulted his texts, he might have been wary of this case. Instead, he contacted his old friend Dr. Sachs, an out-of-town neurosurgeon whom he had used as an expert many times before. The physician was theatrical, articulate, and highly convincing. They often joked that he could convince his own mother that he wasn't her son.

Dr. Sachs was one of a minority of neurosurgeons with a strong preconceived bias against this operation. As a full-time laboratory investigator and medical school professor he hadn't seen a patient in years and had never treated anyone with Leon's injury. However, Dr. Sachs rarely let lack of information or experience interfere with his opinions. There was no doubt in his mind after the briefest case description that Dr. Stanton was grossly negligent and had grievously victimized this poor patient.

He went further. Not only did he feel that the operation was contraindicated, but he insisted that Leon's early neurological progress bore the promise of total recovery. He would probably have walked and returned to his work.

Though momentarily saddened at the tale of this unnecessary injury, Carter was delighted at the analysis. If Leon would have returned to work, then Dr. Stanton was responsible for all lost future income. Dreams of this fortune overshadowed Carter's sorrow about Leon's plight.

Carter took this report to the Klinebergs. Leon, now getting around in a wheelchair under the constant care of a practical nurse, had just returned from his three-month stay in the rehabilitation hospital. His outlook, though far from enthusiastic, was brighter than it had been in the days immediately following the operation. At the hospital he began to work hard again and by now had returned functionally to his preoperation level. His fingers could push the buttons on his electric wheelchair. He could with effort raise his right arm to his mouth and could, once again, hold his own cigarette. He would never walk, and his bladder and bowel controls were lost forever.

The family was overcome by emotion when their suspicions of negligence were confirmed by Carter's report. All of the agony of the injury, the initial signs of improvement, then the crushing defeat of the unsuccessful operation, were relived. When Carter relayed Dr. Sachs' impression that Leon would have recovered completely were it not for the operation, they were livid with fury. A lawsuit could hardly compensate for this egregious crime.

Two days later Carter filed suit in the District Court on behalf of his clients. He asked for $4 million to compensate for lost wages, nursing and hospital costs, pain and suffering, and loss of consortium (the usual comforts of a normal marital relationship). In most cases figures like this were frivolously tossed about. In this instance Carter was convinced that the huge sum was a realistic demand.

Part II—The Trial: Preparation and Litigation

Trial was a long way off, but Andrew Carter knew that his chances for success depended upon careful, comprehensive planning. No detail could be overlooked, no avenue unexplored, no last-minute surprise to catch him unaware. Supported by the strong backing of Dr. Sachs, he was confident of victory and resolved to devote his full energies to this case.

The first order of business was to add several more experts to his attack force. He called Harvey Landon, a neurosurgeon in private practice in Topeka, Kansas, who had helped with other cases. After reviewing the records, Dr. London sent Carter his analysis of the Klineberg case.

"I would have done exactly the same thing for this man," wrote Dr. Landon. "I do these operations all the time. Mr. Klineberg's only hope was to have the operation."

Carter fell back in his chair, stunned. Dr. Landon, after all, was an honest and forthright consultant who freely helped deserving plaintiffs in their lawsuits. This wasn't a case of saying something just to save his fellow doctor.

When another consultant offered the same opinion, Carter turned to the neurosurgery books, unopened until now.

"One of the most controversial areas in neurosurgery."

"A raging debate about operative versus nonoperative management."

". . . A group of patients with a grave prognosis regardless of the therapy."

"No one knows what the right form of treatment is for these patients."

Carter's confidence and faith in this lawsuit was shattered. Dr. Sachs' opinion, he now realized, represented only one voice of a by no means settled controversy. The only thread of hope was the fact that all the authorities agreed "significant" neurological progress meant no operation. He would have to prove, somehow, that Dr. Stanton had operated despite significant progress in Leon Klineberg.

Carter momentarily considered dropping the case, for he was uncertain of Dr. Stanton's guilt. However, he was driven by the forces that direct many plaintiff lawyers—a desire to help this miserable man, the call of the courtroom battle. A tough fight was even more exciting, with a huge verdict awaiting this uncertain victory. Shaken but still determined, he moved forward.

He asked Dr. Sachs to recommend other experts who shared his belief that the operation was improper. Dr. Sachs found two other American physicians and one European authority. All had a strong bias that the operation should never have been performed.

They supported their arguments with carefully selected neurosurgical papers, always eliminating contradictory articles. Two of the four were uncertain about Leon's future without the operation. The other two were sure that he would have walked and would probably have returned to work.

Gradually Carter regained his self-confidence. Although he was still unsure about the merit of his case, he began to feel that he could win regardless of who was right.

Dr. Stanton was deeply distressed when he opened the official envelope and found the formal notification. He was the primary defendant in a malpractice suit. He was surprised but not shocked, since he knew that the Klineberg family was almost inconsolably upset at the outcome of the operation. Furthermore, he had seen many patients with spinal injuries and was attuned to their psychological reactions. Faced with an acute sense of hopelessness, these people frequently seek solace by heaping blame and recriminations upon others—the other participant in the accident, occasionally the doctor. Usually, however, this phase passes with time as the patient resigns himself to his fate and redirects his energies toward his struggle for self-help. For the Klineberg family the period of blame persisted. As Dr. Stanton looked sadly at the legal notice in his hand he had only one regret.

"Why hadn't they discussed this with me? Did I communicate so badly with them? Why was this cold, impersonal piece of paper my first warning of their intention?"

This was his first suit in thirty years of neurosurgical practice—a remarkable record indeed. He thought back over those years with satisfaction. As a resident at the University of Michigan Hospital, one of the best neurosurgery programs of the day, he had been considered outstanding. His current associates admired his surgical skill and judgment. He had all of the attributes of an excellent physician and neurosurgeon, and his sixty-four years had not stolen much of his youthful vigor.

True, some of the newest neurosurgical techniques—delicate microsurgery with instruments viewed with a powerful microscope—had passed him by. Although some of the modern techniques were beyond his reach, he was familiar with all of them. His enthusiasm for learning and his concern for his patients were still his prime motivations. He spent every spare moment reading his journals and absorbing the latest textbooks.

Now, as he pondered the suit notice he thought wryly, "Well, I guess it's about time I got some use out of those $15,000-per-year insurance premiums."

Three days later Gerald Robbins, a vigorous, highly respected trial attorney who did most of the local defense work for doctors, met Dr. Stanton in his office. Their two-hour conference left them both certain that this was a lawsuit that had no valid basis. Dr. Stanton was confident of victory; he knew that he had acted properly.

Robbins, although he felt the case was unjust viewed the problem not through the naïve eyes of a surgeon never before enmeshed in a legal tangle but with the uneasiness of a seasoned trial attorney. His years of experience with malpractice cases told him that fair play and justice do not always win the day. A $4-million lawsuit and a pathetic plaintiff made this a most dangerous and worrisome case.

Robbins consulted his medical advisers. Together they and their neurosurgical experts began the tedious process of building a defense.

The defense experts realized that the treatment of spinal cord injuries was highly controversial. They agreed that neither scientific studies nor other data supported the few outspoken critics of the operation. There were equally talented authorities who were strong proponents of surgery.

To be sure, there were specific, universally accepted indications for surgery: a severe fracture, rapidly deteriorating neurological function, a complete spinal cord block. There was one strong contraindication: significant and continuous improvement from the time of the injury. For the large group of patients who did not fall neatly into any of these categories, opinions differed. Leon, with a partial spinal canal block and apparently arrested neurological progress, occupied this surgical limbo.

The defense experts were an illustrious and impressive group: two medical school department chairmen and two neurosurgeons in a private practice, all actively engaged in the practice of neurosurgery. All could effectively discuss standard care in America. All strongly concurred that Dr. Stanton had not been negligent when he offered and performed surgery upon Leon Klineberg. They agreed that it had been reasonable and in keeping with standard care, under the circumstances, to have performed this operation.

Meanwhile, the lawyers went through the myriad required legal maneuvers—interrogatories, motions, declarations and revised declarations, answers to interrogatories, more interrogatories, and more answers. After almost a year of preliminary jousting they were nearly ready for the main event. In preparation for trial, depositions of all the experts would have to be taken.

These were informal but legally admissible sworn hearings which enabled each side to examine and cross-examine its opponents. Sometimes, as in the case of the European expert, the depositions could be read at trial in lieu of a personal appearance. The surprise witness and sudden revelations, made famous by Perry Mason, were rarities in today's court proceedings. Long before the judge's gavel signaled the start of the trial, each side would have fully surveyed its opponent's ammunition.

The first deposition was held in Europe. Professor Rudolph Hahn had written extensively about spinal injuries. He was renowned but highly controversial. His vehement bias against surgery had made him something of a medical evangelist, although he was respected for his work in rehabilitation.

Because this was the only chance that Robbins would have to question Dr. Hahn (his deposition would be read to the jury), the lawyer methodically pursued every issue in excruciating depth.

"Have you ever practiced medicine in the United States?"

"I was a visiting faculty member of several universities."

"But have you ever actually had your own neurosurgical practice in the United States?"

"No."

(This was a strong plus for the defense for this would weaken this witness's position as a spokesman for standard medical care in Texas.)

"Do you know the standard of care in Texas?"

"Yes."

"How?"

"The entire world has accepted my teaching about this operation and the reasons for not doing it."

"What is your concept of standard care?"

"It is the right way of doing something."

"You mean that your definition of standard care is what you consider to be the correct approach?"

"That is correct."

Robbins was pleased with that answer. Carter was concerned. They both knew that standard care is defined, not by the controversial proclamations of one critic, but by the prevailing practice in that community—what has been accepted and what is done. This witness had effectively disqualified himself as an expert on local American practice. However, the deposition was far from over, and as the examination probed other areas, the witness scored heavily for Leon.

First he alleged that this man would probably have walked and likely have returned to his occupation as an architect. He based that contention on the small amount of movement which returned in the first week. He could speak strongly about this point, for he ran one of the world's largest centers for spine injuries, and he had personally seen thousands of these patients.

Robbins, having scoured the surgical literature prior to this encounter, asked the proper question.

"Can you substantiate that claim with published cases?"

The witness, as Robbins already knew, admitted that he could not.

Finally, after an hour of grueling examination on this

point, the witness admitted that each patient was unique; no one could predict with any degree of certainty what would happen on the basis of early improvement. His impression that Leon would regain function was really nothing more than speculation. This weakened his testimony, but it did not destroy his value, for he remained adamant that his vast experience told him that Leon was destined to recover and that the operation ruined his chances.

His concluding testimony dealt another serious blow to the defense. This distinguished expert felt that Leon showed daily, ever-increasing neurological progress. He had not, as Dr. Stanton argued, reached a plateau. If this were true most authorities, including the defense experts, would concur that surgery was ill advised.

"Upon what do you base that contention, Doctor?" asked Robbins.

"In the first place, let me say that Dr. Stanton did a terrible job of recording his observations of this patient. He wrote occasional notes like 'No change,' but wrote no note at all about neurological findings for one whole week prior to the operation."

"Okay, Doctor, but what I asked you is what makes you say that Mr. Klineberg showed progressive improvement?"

"I learned that from the nurses' notes. For example, this one that says, 'Patient moving better.' I also determined his progress from the observations of the family."

"Doctor, isn't the neurosurgeon a better judge of progress than the family or the nurses?"

"Perhaps, but I can't know what he found if he didn't write any notes."

"Doctor, what if I told you that Dr. Stanton insists that he did examine this man daily and simply did not make records of his neurological findings because there were no changes. He noted several times 'No changes,' and thereafter intended to make a note only if there were significant progress."

"I would say, sir, that this is improper."

"I am not asking you about the quality of the progress notes. I am simply asking you to assume that Dr. Stanton did make such daily determinations and found no change, would that not mean anything to you?"

"Unless it was written down, I don't know if it was true."

Robbins threw up his hands in despair. The witness kept sidestepping his questions. He was so convinced of Dr. Stanton's guilt that he avoided those answers that might weaken his preconceived opinion.

"The family didn't write anything down either, but you believe them and base your entire argument upon their testimony, don't you?"

"Objection, argumentative," interjected Carter. "I'm instructing the witness not to answer."

Try as he would, Robbins could not get the stubborn witness to admit that Dr. Stanton's recollection was as valid as the family's—probably more valid. It was unfortunate that the hospital records were not more complete. Full daily documentation of neurological changes—progress, regression, or no change—would have added support to Dr. Stanton. However, a busy neurosurgeon often does not write complete, ideal notes. Viewed from the vantage point of this lawsuit, the records were imperfect, although they fell within the bounds of usual community practice.

The jury would have to rely on ancillary information to assess neurological change—Dr. Stanton's personal description, the recollection of the family, friends, nurses, and Leon himself, sporadic nurses' notes, and Dr. Stanton's incompletely recorded observations.

Back in the United States the attorneys traveled up the East Coast and across the country to California to interview all the witnesses. Finally, all the opinions were formally recorded and the testimonies tested. The process had been a grueling, laborious task, physically demanding and financially straining. Both Leon Klineberg and the opposing insurance company had spent $60,000 in legal costs, travel expenses, and expert witness fees. But each side, knowing what a high-priced reward lay at the end of this case, was strongly committed to winning. It was imposssible for the case to be settled out of court, since both sides believed they were right. The insurance company would not pay a staggering settlement in a case it believed unfounded.

The majority of the plaintiff witnesses supported Dr. Hahn's basic contentions. Only Dr. Sachs believed as strongly that Leon would have walked again; the others confessed that their experience with this type of injury was more limited, but they felt the operation was ill advised. Only one of them could properly speak about standards of care—a practicing neurosurgeon from Wisconsin. The others were either long retired or involved in research and teaching, far removed from the daily decisions of clinical practice. All three of those witnesses, well drilled before the depositions, interpreted the scattered records and Leon's personal statement as indicative of continuous, unarrested clinical progress. This was the most damaging testimony of all.

The defense witnesses took a different position. They all concurred that although some muscle strength increased for the first two weeks, this was the inevitable consequence of persistent exercise and reflex activity. There was no evidence of new motor function. They were unanimous in their contentions that Dr. Stanton's observations far outweighed those of the biased and medically naïve family. Admittedly, Dr. Stanton's notes were incomplete, but the statements of Leon, his family, and the surgeon convinced the defense witnesses that their opinions were well founded.

All these witnesses were well qualified to discuss standard care. They firmly asserted that, despite the claims of their European colleague, the standards in this country had not uniformly followed his direction. Many centers, including their own university hospitals, readily operated on patients with injuries and a clinical course exactly like Mr. Klineberg's. Their assertions steadfastly resisted erosion by Carter's legal and semantic efforts. He confronted four convincing spokesmen who unanimously believed that the operation was appropriate.

The defense witnesses argued strongly that Leon would probably not have walked and would surely not have returned to his previous occupation. They cited many reputable articles which illustrated grave prognosis in this type of injury. Although there was a possibility of significant improvement, the chances were small. Leon was almost surely doomed to a life in a wheelchair with or without the operation. Obviously this could hurt Leon's case, for on this point, it was a question of whom the jury would believe—the plaintiff or defense experts. The defense experts had better credentials and, more importantly, the weight of reputable medical publications supporting their positions.

As the countdown for trial began, Mr. Carter's anxiety grew. Expenses in trial preparation had already reached the $80,000 mark. There were only two things in his favor. First, the strong contention by his experts and the family that neurological progress had not ceased. This would have to be exploited to its fullest extent. Second, the pathetic situation of Leon Klineberg, forever confined to the wheelchair—a talented man reduced to a helpless, hopeless burden. He would have to pick the jury with unusual care and skill. He must find six sympathetic jurors.

Ironically, both sides were pleased with the jury selection. This mutual satisfaction bore striking witness to the mysteries of jury motivations. No one really knows what makes juries tick, though there are many self-proclaimed experts. Four of the six jurors were college graduates. The defense was pleased, since this might enable them to better understand the complex medical situation. Full understanding would inevitably lead to a successful defense. Three were women. Carter was delighted, since it would be easiest to sway them with the emotional appeal.

Judge Halstead, an experienced, middle-aged jurist, approached the bench. The opposing parties and the few onlookers rose. The judge would play an important role in the trial. His discretion and knowledge of the law would be called upon time and time again. He would have to admit or reject testimony, to rule on admissibility of evidence, and, finally and most important, to instruct the jury just before their deliberations. The jury's understanding of the legal requirements in this type of case would depend largely upon his instructions.

Judge Halstead was a competent trial judge, but he had little experience with medical malpractice. The defense attorneys were concerned about this, because the strength of their case lay in the fact that the burden of proof was on the plaintiff. The defendant was innocent until proven guilty. It was up to the plaintiff to prove that something improper was done and that Leon would have walked if the untimely operation had not intervened. The defense attorneys were convinced that if those instructions were properly provided the jury would have to find Dr. Stanton innocent. If they were not given correctly, emotionalism and nonlegal considerations would have freer reign. Unchecked, his personal, pathetic appeal could win Leon's case.

The first day was taken up by the jury selection and some preliminary instructions. The substance of the trial began the second day as the plaintiff presented his case.

Carter's first witnesses were members of the family and some of the attending nurses. They all testified that Leon was improving day by day—always gaining more strength and greater neurological function. Robbins jumped to the defense. He would have to minimize the importance of this potentially damaging testimony by pointing out discrepancies in testimony and convincing the jury that these observations of nonphysician witnesses are unreliable. Understandably, the family and the nurses hoped beyond hope for any sign of improvement. They are easily swayed by the slightest hint of movement, reflex, or voluntary motion into believing that the patient is improving dramatically. Moreover, thought Robbins, how can one put stock in the testimony of the very people who stand to win a fortune from a favorable verdict? Would they be expected to say that their dear husband or father was a goner and this lawsuit was a waste of time? Robbins would establish that the neurosurgeon is the one who must make those decisions and that neurological progress must be dramatic before the operation is denied.

Carter repeatedly asked his witnesses, "Are you certain that there was daily progress with no plateau?"

All responded, "Yes."

Robbins demanded a detailed description of that progress.

"Exactly what could Mr. Klineberg do? What muscles did he move? How much strength did he have? How did you test that strength?"

Each witness related a slightly different story. None of them had made specific tests. All of them just had the impression that there was improvement.

"Have you ever had any prior experience evaluating a patient with this type of injury?"

"No" was the uniform response. Robbins felt that he had pointed out the poor foundation of the testimony, despite their obvious sincerity. However, his experience cautioned him to be wary. Juries can relate in a personal way to such lay observers—their nonmedical colleagues. Impugning their observations and their descriptions is like accusing every jury member of being incapable of recognizing simple facts.

The fifth witness was Leon's nineteen-year-old son. He had visited his father almost every day and, like the others, testified that there was continued and relentless improvement in neurological function. But his testimony was far stronger. He had specific recollection of his father's movements and stated that he made some specific tests.

"How did you test your father's motion?"

"I placed small weights, fishing sinkers, on the fingers of his right hand and had him lift them one at a time. The first week he could lift them about one inch off the bed, but by the end of the third week he could move each finger individually about two or three inches."

"Was it your impression that he would regain total use of that hand?" Carter asked, although he knew this was an improper question.

"Objection–the witness is not qualified to testify about prognosis," Robbins quickly interjected.

"Sustained," nodded Judge Halstead. "You know that's an improper question, Mr. Carter."

"Did anyone see you perform these tests?" asked Robbins.

"No."

"Did you tell anyone about them?"

"I may have mentioned them to my mother."

"How about Dr. Stanton?"

"I didn't have much chance to see Dr. Stanton."

"But didn't you think this was important enough to let the doctor know about it?"

"I figured that he knew what he was doing and that he would do the same sort of tests. I was sure that he must be aware of my father's improvement."

Robbins felt a sharp pang–this testimony was hurting his client's case severely. For although the son was a lay witness, he made an honest impression while relating these specific motor tests. The jury's eyes were riveted on this pleasant-looking young man who obviously had spent many long, devoted hours with the ailing father he loved. Robbins could see their believing that if he saw those fingers move the way he said they did, they probably moved.

The plaintiff's neurological experts followed the family on the witness stand. Robbins vigorously objected to reading the testimony of the European expert. He argued that this man was unfamiliar with the standard of care in Texas and that his testimony was, therefore, inadmissible. The judge disagreed, citing the liberal admission of testimony from faraway experts commonly accepted in that state. Robbins capitulated, but made a mental note that this might be something that could be used later if they lost and had to appeal the case.

Carter's experts adhered to their preliminary testimonies. All of them felt that the operation was ill advised, even if a neurological plateau had been reached. As far as they were concerned, no competent neurosurgeon would have operated.

On cross-examination, Robbins continually emphasized his strong points. It was his job to try to impeach these witnesses. If he could show that their testimonies differed from that of all of his highly qualified experts, he could, he hoped, minimize their impact.

"Are you saying that there is not a respectable school of thought among neurosurgeons in this country that recommends operation for this type of patient?"

"Not anymore," replied the highly polished medical school professor.

"When was the last time you performed such an operation, sir?"

"At least fifteen years ago, because I think they are dangerous."

He cleverly dealt a blow of his own in that qualifying clause, but Robbins recovered.

"When was the last time you personally did any operation?"

"About ten years ago."

"So you are not engaged in the practice of neurosurgery?"

"I teach residents neurosurgery."

"But you do not have a private practice of your own, with your own patients and doing your own operations, do you?"

"No."

The professor's ability to speak of standard care in the community was being attacked by Robbins, but although the attorney knew that a practicing physician who saw this type of patient often should be the best spokesman regarding standard care, much of this escaped the jury. They saw an articulate board-certified neurosurgeon—a teacher in a university medical center. To them, the nuances of private practice and standard care, major points in the law, were very subtle indeed. Although the professor could offer no factual support for his contention that Leon would have returned to work, his opinion withstood a strong cross-examination.

The final plaintiff witnesses were the plaintiffs themselves—Leon and his wife. Leon was a pathetic figure. He sat almost motionless in his wheelchair. He could move one of his hands well enough to control the buttons that moved his chair, but he could do little else. Carter extracted every ounce of pity from the jury. He showed in grim detail Leon's utter helplessness and hopelessness—like a baby but worse, for a baby had a bright future. Mrs. Klineberg testified that she dressed him in the morning, brushed his teeth, irrigated his urinary catheter, awoke hourly throughout the night to turn him so that he would not get any bedsores, and often manually extracted his bowel movements, which frequently became hard and impacted.

At this description, juror No. 6's head reeled with a sudden and dreadful recollection of a personal experience, long forgotten, vividly revived by this poignant narration. Her aged, helpless mother, a stroke victim for fifteen years, was back in her arms. Shaken, the juror gradually regained her composure, but now with a profound empathy for this tragic witness. She knew that, for her, the future was a living death.

Carter introduced pictures of his client showing that he had been a vigorously athletic man who jogged every day and lifted weights. For him, his helplessness was particularly painful. Carter could see that his carefully orchestrated emotional appeal was working. It was clear from the sympathy on every juror's face that they felt the daily misery of this hapless man. Several decided to do anything they could to help this miserable man—this poor victim of a doctor's knife!

The first six days of the trial belonged to the plaintiff. Now the defense would have its turn.

One by one the witnesses raised their right hands.

"Do you solemnly swear . . . ?"

"I do."

"State you name and your qualifications."

There was no doubt that these four men were highly qualified neurosurgeons.

"Do you think that Dr. Stanton deviated from expected standard care?"

"No."

"Do you think that the operation was indicated and that it was performed correctly?"

"Yes. In fact, Dr. Stanton could have been sued if he had not operated on this man."

"Objection," claimed Carter, "conjectural."

"Do you think that Mr. Klineberg would have walked or practiced architecture again if he had not had this operation?"

"Of course, we can never be 100 percent certain in these cases, but considering the severity of this injury, the small amount of progress shown initially and the patient's advanced age, it is highly unlikely. He would almost surely have had a major and permanent neurological deficit no matter what."

Each witness was asked to describe in detail the anatomy of the spinal cord and the extent of this injury. Two of them skillfully drew colored pictures for the jury as they carefully gave them an anatomy lesson as they would a class of first-year medical students. Each described his experience with this type of injury, and the bad results that almost invariably followed.

The preliminary answers were in: both surgical and nonsurgical practices were prevalent in the community; neither seemed to be superior to the other. It was impossible to accurately predict the prognosis, but patients like Leon generally did poorly. Full recovery, a miraculous occurrence, was rarely more than an unfulfilled dream.

Following each direct interrogation by Robbins of his eminent witnesses, Carter conducted his cross-examination. He was a clever and seasoned attorney who had that important trial sense that permitted him to concentrate on the few helpful issues, brushing the complex and damaging points aside. The strong opposing testimony tarnished his experts' arguments that this operation should never be performed. His one strength, besides sympathy for Leon's condition, was the testimony of the family that this man was making striking progress. Not one of the defense witnesses could deny that significant progress was a stong contraindication to operation. He would emphasize and reemphasize that testimony.

Carter took aim at the first defense expert, a neurosurgery department chairman.

"What if I told you, sir, that this man was making significant progress?"

"I don't believe that there was significant progress," replied the physician.

"Well, sir," continued Carter, "we have had testimony in this courtroom that Mr. Klineberg was progressing day by day in an uninterrupted and advancing manner. Assuming that this were true, would the operation have been well advised?"

Avoiding this legal trap, the witness replied, "I would have to know exactly what you mean by 'significant,' and who made the determination of that finding."

"The son stated that he tested Mr. Klineberg's finger motion with weights and that he could move each finger individually like this," he demonstrated.

Having lived through many agonizing months with hopeful families, friends, and nurses and having been misled on many occasions by their optimistic discoveries, the scholarly physician was undaunted by this revelation.

"The neurosurgeion is the only person who can accurately evaluate these problems. Family, friends, nurses, all have high hopes and expectations. They are not trained to recognize true neurological progress, and they regard any apparent change as meaningful. There are many movements, for example, that are involuntary reflex movements which have no functional meaning. Lay observers often see those as 'significant' and hopeful signs of progress."

Carter ignored this comment, hoping to minimize its jury impact.

"But, Doctor," he persisted, "would individual voluntary finger movements with weights attached to those fingers be considered 'reflex actions'?"

"I suppose not."

"And, Doctor, wouldn't you consider these fine finger movements that I described to you indicative of significant neurological progress?"

"Those movements that you described, Mr. Carter, were not 'fine finger movements.' The muscle groups that control those movements are in the forearm. The small muscles in the hand that control fine grasp and bringing the fingers together are what I would call 'fine movements.' "

"All right, Doctor, but wouldn't you agree that this represented significant neurological progress?"

"It might, but again, I would point out that the lay observer is a poor judge of this type of function—particularly a family member."

The look of disgusted disbelief that crossed the face of juror No. 2 was not missed by Carter. He was successfully making his point that even lay observers can see progress.

"Doctor, wouldn't you agree that if a patient were making significant progress, operation should be avoided?"

"Yes, that is well accepted."

Carter was overjoyed. He had extracted a statement—repeatedly qualified, to be sure—that if the son's observations were indeed accurate, this could be a sign of significant progress and might militate against operation. The doctor's disparagement of lay versus medical evaluation could be dealt with in Carter's appeal to the jury. After all, he would argue that they were all laymen, and couldn't they recognize a simple action like finger movement?

That night the remaining defense experts met with Robbins and Dr. Stanton. They were not permitted to discuss the testimony of other experts, but they could consider trial tactics and the direction of the plaintiff attorney. They could also bc apprised of the son's testimony so that they could, at their leisure, consider answers to Carters' questions. All believed very strongly that the lay observer should be discounted unless his observations are confirmed by the attending physician, but all confessed that the movements described by the son could, if confirmed by the neurosurgeon, signify progress. Dr. Stanton insisted that no such progress existed.

The expected line of questioning followed in droning repetition. The defense stressed over and over that the neurosurgeon was in the best position to evaluate his patient; that the decision to operate must be his; that the operation, according to all hospital records, was proper and timely, and that without it there would have been little hope for useful recovery.

Carter leaned heavily on the family's testimony, repeatedly underscoring the argument that the observed finger movement could signify progress if those observations were accurate.

Throughout the trial, all of the attorneys kept their eyes riveted on the jury. Were they making an impression? Were their witnesses coming through? Each side felt that its appeal was strong. Carter was convinced that the son's testimony, coupled with support by his experts and the miserable lot of his client, could win the day. The defense strongly believed that its position was right and that its illustrious experts made a convincing jury appeal. Robbins retained an underlying anxiety, however, since emotional sentiment in a case like this heavily favors the plaintiff.

The last day saw each of the attorneys squaring off with their final arguments. While earnestly searching the faces of the six jurors they summed up the proceedings of the two previous weeks, vigorously emphasizing the points in their favor and skirting those areas in which their cases were weak.

Attorney Carter had carefully chosen his suit that morning: a moderately conservative gray wool, worn with a pale-blue shirt and navy tie. He knew that he made an attractive appearance. His youth was softened by the conservatism of his gray suit, but the blue of his shirt and tie heightened the blue of his eyes. His dress, his stance, and his gestures were calculated to make him appear earnest, concerned, and sympathetic. As he stood confidently before them he thought he saw in their eyes approval and empathy. He began.

"Ladies and gentlemen of the jury, we have shown that this unfortunate man was the victim of medical malpractice. That had it not been for the intervention of this ill-advised operation, he would have regained useful and probably normal function. We have heard the testimony of his family that his progress was continuing unchecked. We have also heard the other side and the defendant, Dr. Stanton, state that this was not so and that a layman cannot accurately assess this type of progress.

"I ask you, ladies and gentlemen, who among you cannot tell when someone is moving his fingers? Do you really believe that it takes four years of medical school to tell when someone is moving his fingers? Nowhere in Dr. Stanton's poor and incomplete hospital notes does he specifically discuss finger motion. He doesn't say that the fingers were not moving, but we have here a witness who says that they were. Not only that, but this witness"—he carefully avoided referring to him as the plaintiff's son—"performed the specific tests to assess those movements by putting weights on the fingers. No expert can say that this was not a test of voluntary finger movement. . . ."

Next Carter selectively recapitulated the testimony of the European expert who was most committed to the concept of full recovery.

"Ladies and gentlemen, you have heard read into evidence the deposition of Dr. Hahn, the eminent European neurosurgeon and scholar who has followed the progress of three thousand patients with cervical-spine injuries. You have heard his contention that Mr. Klineberg would regain full neurological function if this improper operation had not intervened. Others have denied this, but none of them have the extensive experience of this world authority. I ask you to accept the benefit of his experience and to conclude that the only thing which interrupted Mr. Klineberg's progress toward full and complete recovery was this disastrous operation. . . . The plaintiff rests."

Now it was Robbins' turn. An older, less handsome man than Carter, Robbins was somewhat less concerned about his appearance. Nevertheless, his dark-blue pin-stripe had been cleaned and pressed for the final arguments. The technique he decided to cultivate with this jury was that of a sympathetic, understanding man, able to appreciate the helpless, hopeless life Mr. Klineberg was destined to lead, but not willing to allow anyone to blame Dr. Stanton for that fate.

He recounted one by one the testimonies of his witnesses.

He reiterated their belief that the neurosurgeon, not a biased family member, was the only proper judge of improvement. He indicated that only two of the plaintiff experts felt that this man was on his way to complete recovery; the other seven experts (five defense and two plaintiff) did not. He read excerpts from medical literature which confirmed a poor prognosis. He asked why, if the European expert was so adamant about the probable success of nonoperative treatment, wasn't he able to produce any literature to support his position. Dr. Hahn had been studying these patients for thirty years, yet his impression that Leon would walk again remained an unsupported conjecture. After one and a half hours of low-key but eloquent appeal to the jury, he concluded.

"The defense rests."

Judge Halstead's all-important charge to the jury was the final act of this protracted confrontation. Robbins, in an earlier conference, asked that the judge fully expound upon the legal requirements of proof and causation. He wanted to be certain that the jury completely understood its responsibility: that the six-member panel be well prepared to analyze these complex issues with a minimum of emotionalism and a maximum of legal sophistication. Of course, it was impossible to give a jury a legal education in thirty minutes, but its fundamental duties could be explained. He asked that Judge Halstead inform the jury that the burden of proof in this and any other case rests with the plaintiff—that a man is innocent until proven guilty.

It was the responsibility of the plaintiff to prove that Dr. Stanton deviated from expected community standards and that in all probability that deviation caused a serious injury. In other words, unless it were proven that Leon would probably have walked and returned to work had there been no operation, then Dr. Stanton could not be held responsible for his permanent and disabling injury.

Robbins felt that if the jury were properly instructed and if thcy heeded these instructions, his client would have to win the case. At the very worst he might lose a small sum, but never the $4 million demanded by the Klineberg family as compensation for lost income. Surely the jury, after all the expert testimony, could never believe that Leon Klineberg might have recovered enough to return to his occupation as an architect.

The elderly judge instructed the jury about reviewing the evidence. He told them that they must put all emotional considerations aside—admittedly a superhuman feat—and that they must decide the case purely on the basis of facts and the testimony presented to them. Robbins folded and unfolded his hands, anxiously awaiting the strong and clear instructions that never came. Judge Halstead gave the jury some general information about the necessary relationship between negligence and injury, but his description was weak. He failed to leave the jury with a clear understanding that they could hold Dr. Stanton responsible for the paralysis only if they truly believed that Mr. Klineberg was on his way to probable recovery prior to the operation.

Part III—The Verdict

Negligence, proximate cause, injury—those three universal principles of a medical malpractice case were now awaiting the deliberation and decision of the jury. Before eavesdropping on the discussion in the jury room, let us carry out our own analysis—an analysis based solely on the facts and expert testimony; the kind that a panel of medical and legal experts would make.

First, was Dr. Stanton negligent? Did he perform an operation that most of his colleagues would have avoided?

The majority of defense experts, all eminent authorities, testified that to operate or not to operate upon patients with these spinal injuries is a difficult decision to make, uncertain at best. Both approaches are readily accepted by competent neurosurgeons in a patient with a severe spinal cord injury whose progress has plateaued. The books and published articles all agree, with a slight majority favoring surgery.

Thus the dissenting experts who supported Leon were spokesmen for a minority viewpoint. Their strong pleas against operation were not indicative of standard surgical care. Consequently, assuming that Leon did not make significant progress prior to the operation, the operation was not negligent.

Since all of the experts agreed that significant progress would contraindicate an operation, the reconstruction of Leon's first three hospital weeks is of paramount importance. Despite the protests of Carter and the Klineberg family, the neurosurgeon must be the one to judge daily progress. The family and other laymen, hopeful for any favorable signs and unschooled in the highly sophisticated intricacies of a neurolgical examination, are not reliable observers of progress. Watchful inspection of the patient, daily assessment of change, and the final decision to operate must rest with the person in charge. An expert panel of physicians and lawyers would never base a conviction in a case as complex as this one on the word of one family member against that of the doctor.

Even if Dr. Stanton were found guilty of malpractice —even if it were decided that the operation was ill advised—the damage value would be small. Leon was essentially a quadraplegic—paralyzed in all four extremities by the injuries his spinal cord sustained in the automobile accident. All of the published reports and all of the testimony, except that of two plaintiff experts, confirmed a grim prognosis. Since Leon was already doomed to a life as an invalid, Dr. Stanton could hardly have substantially worsened that fate. After all, he ultimately regained all the function he had prior to surgery. Perhaps without the operation Leo would have been able to move his leg a bit higher or close his fingers more tightly. Maybe he would have been able to help his wife in her hourly tasks of turning him and her frequent chore of transferring him to and from his wheelchair. Would he ever have walked again? Most likely not. Would he ha e returned to work? Extremely doubtful. Therefore, even if Dr. Stanton were found guilty, he was responsible for very minimal injury. He was not to blame for this man's lifelong disability, nor was he the cause of Leon's inability to work again.

Even if it found him guilty an impartial panel, after reviewing all of the facts and weighing the evidence, would award no more than $200,000. This would be the amount required to compensate for the operation itself and for the slight increase in disability.

That is the way an impartial panel made up of doctors and lawyers might analyze the facts of a case. Let us now turn to the actual deliberations carried on by the lay jury.

The jury deliberation began at 1 P.M. on Friday. First came a preliminary vote.

"Clearly not guilty," concluded jurors 1, 3, and 5.

"You must be kidding," exclaimed the other three almost simultaneously.

The hope of an early decision, the weekend Little League games, picnics with the families, or catching up on some of that neglected garden work quickly faded. It would be a protracted debate.

"How can we possibly find him guilty?" asked the young engineer who occupied spot No. 1 in the jury box. "All of those neurosurgeons testified that Mr. Klineberg was the victim of his accident. That his chances of walking again were almost nil. That the operation was reasonable. That it was his only hope."

"We all know that doctors will say anything to protect their fellow doctors," responded No. 2, a woman juror. "What did you expect them to say? Several experts opposed Dr. Stanton. Isn't their testimony worth much more than the self-protective protests of fellow neurosurgeons?"

Juror No. 3, a middle-aged woman, was unconvinced.

"I think you are being a little unfair. Those men seemed honest and truly committed to their points of view. I don't think that you can say they supported the doctor just because they wanted to help him. I think they believed what they said."

"They may have believed most of what they said," came the forceful reply, "when Mr. Carter asked them if they would have done exactly the same thing in this case, most of them gave us that old bit about 'appropriate and standard.' I don't think any of them would have operated on that man."

"I didn't get that impression at all," interjected juror No. 5. "I think you're trying to play psychoanalyst by reading too much between the lines. I don't think any of them really knew what he would have done because he wasn't there making the decision. The lesson I learned from them was that this is a difficult decision to make that can only be made by the treating neurosurgeon. So standard and appropriate care is important. It says that Dr. Stanton acted properly."

"Well, I think you're awfully gullible if you let those experts fool you," retorted No. 2, "but even if we admit that sometimes these operations are performed and properly so, we're still left with a serious mistake in this particular case. All of the experts, for both sides, said that if Mr. Klineberg's progress was good, no operation. You heard what the family, especially the son, said about his progress. Even some of the defense experts admitted, however reluctantly, that those fingers moving one by one might be significant."

"I agree wholeheartedly," interjected juror No. 6. "That poor family. That ruined man. That miserable, unhappy woman. We must help them. We have to do what we can!" Those years of personal anguish as constant guardian to an invalid forced this entreaty from deep within her.

"We're not Robin Hood," protested juror No. 1. "Our job is not to rob from the rich and give to this unfortunate man just because he has an injury. We have to decide that Dr. Stanton was responsible."

"That's right. And about those finger movements, all the experts said that the family couldn't accurately judge those fine points of improvement," added juror No. 3.

"Oh, come on! Any of us knows that's a lot of bull. You mean to tell me that you or I can't tell when someone's fingers are moving? Don't be ridiculous."

"I agree," added No. 6. "They must think we're all stupid not to know when fingers are moving."

"But how can we trust the family's interpretation? We know they are prejudiced, if not by hopes for Mr. Klineberg's improvement, then certainly by the prospects of this large amount of money that they may win," snapped juror No. 5.

"And Dr. Stanton is equally driven by his desire to win this lawsuit. He is no more believable than the family, and since he didn't write anything in the chart during the hospitalization, how can we believe now that Mr. Klineberg remained totally paralyzed at that time? The family related specific and definite movements, including a detailed description of that whole fancy maneuver with weights on the fingers," retorted juror No. 2.

"But why didn't they mention that to Dr. Stanton?"

"Who knows what goes through people's minds during those trying times? They probably thought that Dr. Stanton knew what was happening but still thought the operation was necessary. They trusted him. A misplaced trust, I might add." Juror No. 2, a highly articulate spokeswoman, was adamant. She was convinced of Dr. Stanton's guilt and was determined to capture the opinions of her three dissenting cohorts.

The debate raged through the night. By midnight, when they retired to their homes, jurors 3 and 5 had changed their preliminary opinions and reluctantly corroborated Dr. Stanton's guilt. Juror No. 1 was the only holdout when the jury reconvened the next morning.

He resisted the early-morning barrage, this time by all of the other jurors. He could not easily consider the strong testimony of the defense witnesses as slanted attempts to save their colleague! But as the morning dragged on his staunch protests weakened. By noon he had capitulated.

"Well, maybe you're right. If all of you really believe what the family said, maybe I'm being unfairly skeptical. I guess I'll go along with you."

The decision was now unanimous. Dr. Stanton was guilty of malpractice.

These six jurors, none of whom had ever seen a cervical spinal cord, let alone this neurosurgical operation, together agreed that Dr. Stanton had made a serious mistake when he operated on Leon Klineberg. Having established Dr. Stanton's guilt, the jury would begin the second stage of their deliberation. It was up to them to decide how much money should be given to the victim.

Naturally, the cost of the extensive hospital stay, some of the rehabilitation expenses, and some compensation for pain and suffering would be borne by Dr. Stanton and his insurance company. Those damages were minor compared to more serious decisions which faced this jury. Would they hold Dr. Stanton responsible for Klineberg's lost income? Could they possibly believe that he would have returned to work if nature, unimpeded by the surgeon's knife, had taken its course?

Judge Halstead's instructions to the jury were weak on this point. He had failed to inform them that the burden of proof rests with the plaintiff to establish in all medical probability that he would have recovered fully. That is to say, the plaintiff must prove through expert testimony that Leon Klineberg would not only have walked again but would have returned to work as an architect.

Instead, he permitted the jury to begin its debate with only a hint of its legal responsibilities. Of course, it is possible that even the most detailed instructions would not have altered this jury's decision.

Juror No. 1, with residual sympathy for Dr. Stanton, began.

"It seems to me that we can't give this man much money. He probably would never have walked again anyway and surely wouldn't have returned to work. Even if Dr. Stanton shouldn't have operated and even if that operation made Mr. Klineberg worse, it certainly didn't make him much worse. Dr. Stanton is simply not responsible for this whole injury —this paralysis. We can only give Mr. Klineberg enough money to pay for the negative effects of the operation, and what is that? Moving one arm a little less, lifting his leg slightly less?"

"That's absurd!" snapped juror No. 2, ever the plaintiff advocate. "Dr. Sachs, the university professor, and Dr. Hahn, the famous authority who has taken care of hundreds of patients like this, said he would have returned to work. Besides, if this poor man was injured at all by that no-good neurosurgeon he should be completely repaid. No amount of money could be enough."

"I am just not sure," added juror No. 3. "Even two of the plaintiff's own witnesses didn't really think that Mr. Klineberg was going to return to work, and all of the defense witnesses thought that was very unlikely. That makes it seven to two against any chance for complete recovery. Also, all of these articles that we have here say that the chances are very poor."

Juror No. 1 nodded his assent.

"But none of them was as experienced as Dr. Hahn," returned No. 2.

Juror No. 4 puffed his pipe thoughtfully. "I have to agree with that. I think that we must have the strength of our convictions. We have agreed that the operation was improper and that Mr. Klineberg did get worse afterward. I think we're nitpicking when we talk about whether or not he would have walked or worked again. Dr. Stanton screwed up, and he should pay for this injury."

"I may be mistaken," responded No. 1, "but don't we

have to show that Dr. Stanton was responsible for the paralysis before we make him shell out a fortune?"

"I say it makes no difference—and besides, he was," answered No. 2.

"Anyway, it's the insurance company that pays, and they have a lot more money than poor Mr. Klineberg will in a few years. Did you see how pathetic he and his family looked?"

Again, juror No. 6 recalled those years that seemed like an eternity when she nursed her stricken mother.

"That poor wife needs help. She must be given enough money to give her some relief. They've got to be able to pay for nurses so that woman can get away some of the time. That poor miserable woman!" She was almost in tears.

"I thought that Mr. Robbins was downright nasty and rude to the witnesses, and especially to Mr. Klineberg," interjected juror No. 5 in her only comment of the day.

"Yes, and he seemed awfully self-satisfied, but that handsome Mr. Carter was the picture of concern. I believe he really cares about that poor man and his family."

Progressively the arguments deteriorated from matters of law and legal responsibilities to comments about the rich insurance companies, overcharging doctors, and the demeanor and even clothing of the opposing counsels. Try as he would, juror No. 1, supported slightly by No. 3, was unable to redirect the discussion. Even they were uncertain of their responsibilities, since their instructions from the judge had been sketchy. They felt that they should not award a great deal of money, but their abilities to articulate the reasons faltered as the hours passed. After three days of grueling debate jurors No. 1 and 3 finally agreed with their comrades that the rich insurance company could afford a loss far more than Leon and his family could afford another setback. They would return a handsome verdict.

A hush fell over the courtroom as the jury shuffled into their assigned seats. The visitors' gallery, empty during the three-week trial period except for an occasional family member or class of local students observing justice in action, was now filled to capacity. All the law partners from the plaintiff and defense firms, the friends and relatives of Leon Klineberg and of Dr. Stanton, as well as reporters who had been alerted that a verdict for the plaintiff could bring a record $4 million, eagerly awaited the decision.

"All rise," announced the gravel-voiced bailiff who had dutifully guarded the courtroom for so long that he felt it was his personal possession. Judge Halstead marched to the bench with studied dignity, sat down, and pounded his gavel.

"District Court is now in session in the case of Klineberg versus Stanton."

"Has the jury reached its verdict?" Judge Halstead wasted no time getting down to business.

"We have, your honor," replied juror No. 1, the foreman. "We find Dr. Stanton guilty as charged."

The faces of Robbins and Dr. Stanton fell simultaneously. Carter smiled broadly at his clients.

"What damage award have you determined?" asked Judge Halstead.

"Two million, thirty thousand dollars," responded juror No. 1.

A wave of emotion rocked the courtroom. Horrified gasps erupted from Dr. Stanton's side; laughter and cheers from Leon's supporters. Carter embraced the Klinebergs.

Dr. Stanton slumped back into his seat.

"How could they find me guilty? And how could they give him that much money?" he moaned to his attorney. "I was just trying to do my best for him. They must have believed that S.O.B. witness who said he'd go back to work."

He fought hard to suppress the emotional breakdown welling up within him.

"What am I going to do? I only have one and a half million dollars' worth of insurance. Where can I get the five hundred thousand?"

Mr. Robbins tried to console him.

"Don't worry, it's not all over. There are many grounds for appeal. This was the worst verdict I have ever heard."

Dr. Stanton had just learned a terrible and agonizing lesson. Jurors are swayed by many factors other than the evidence: the appeal of opposing counsel, emotional feelings toward the plaintiff, personal experiences with helpless relatives, mistrust of doctors and negative attitudes toward insurance companies. To jurors testimony from lay witnesses—people like themselves—may be more convincing than that of the greatest authorities, automatically suspect since they belong to the medical fraternity. They assess the same facts as a panel composed of doctors and lawyers, but jury members are profoundly influenced by pressures and feelings apart from the medical or legal realities of the case.

Misguided decisions by juries and unrealistically high damage verdicts have contributed to a national crisis over medical malpractice. Malpractice suits have led to serious economic problems and to dangerous changes in the distribution and nature of medical care. The next chapters will delineate the problems that face our country and the decisions and solutions that may someday solve them.

10

The Tidal Wave

Malpractice claims have skyrocketed in the past two decades. Today physicians and their insurers are engulfed by a wave of litigation that has harmed them and the public alike. Recriminations from all sides, mounting health care costs, the possibility of chaotic solutions, and ultimately, suffering for the American consumer have emerged from the current turmoil.

Legal considerations and costs of insurance protection are increasingly dictating the practice of medicine. Physicians pay approximately $1 billion annually for insurance premiums. Hospitals and pharmaceutical companies pay even more. These costs are distributed among all of us in the form of higher physicians' fees, increased hospital charges, and more expensive drugs. Moreover, malpractice fears have driven physicians toward "defensive medicine"—the ordering of unnecessary laboratory studies—which costs between one and seven billion wasted dollars every year.

These legal problems pose an even more dangerous threat to medicine. They have begun to undermine and redirect the distribution of medical care, the availability of certain specialists, and even the fundamental manner in which medicine is practiced. Insurance premiums of up to $50,000 per year have driven some specialists out of high-risk urban areas, have forced semiretired or part-time practitioners out of practice, and have kept newly trained specialists from starting their practices in some locations. New standards of medical practice have arisen, not in response to medical realities or patient needs, but from the pervasive fear of litigation. Doctor-patient rapport has been dealt a final blow by this atmosphere—a blow that has struck effective patient care as well.

Some argue that the threat of malpractice litigation improves health care. In one sense this is true. It mandates tighter controls and surveillance of hospital and office practice, and this undoubtedly has improved certain standards. But uplifting standards by threats of lawsuits is like improving social behavior by public whippings. It offers a measure of symptomatic improvement, but it introduces its own anxieties and ignores the fundamental problems.

This is not a plea against malpractice litigation. Patients who are wronged have a moral and legal right to redress for their injuries. At the same time that these victims are being compensated, however, there must be a concerted effort to examine and attack the roots of malpractice. Moreover, the system must be changed so that only deserving claimants are rewarded, rather than the self-defeating trend to compensate all plaintiffs, regardless of merit.

INSURANCE COSTS

Insurance premiums for doctors, hospitals, and pharmaceutical companies, as well as the expense of excessive "protective" laboratory studies, costs the American consumer between $2 and $8 billion per year. Yet despite staggering premiums, most malpractice insurance carriers cannot keep pace with claims.

Defending a malpractice case costs thousands of dollars, no matter how minor the claim. Attorneys and expert medical witnesses must review the records, prepare supporting medical arguments, and spend time in depositions, pretrial meetings, and trial. At $50 to $200 per hour for each professional participant, the fees rapidly mount up. For this reason many companies prefer to settle a case, regardless of merit, for $5,000 or $10,000 rather than bear the burden of litigation. This practice, although financially sound in a given case, is self-defeating in the long run for it encourages more and more groundless claims.

The proliferation of settlements for good and bad cases costs millions of dollars. Moreover, cases won by the plaintiff at trial are bringing higher and higher verdict awards, far outstripping the general inflationary rate. Now $1-million recoveries, newsworthy before the middle 1960s, are becoming commonplace. Because of these economic pressures, insurance companies have frequently had to raise their premiums. Increases of 100 to 700 percent have received headline attention in medical periodicals and national newspapers, and these have driven up the costs of medical care. A New York orthopedic surgeon recently noted that his fees were increased by $56 per patient to cover his staggering $50,000-per-year premium. From $5 to $10 per day is added to the cost of hospital care to cover their liability insurance.

Malpractice insurance premiums are individualized according to specialty and geographical location. Most physicians pay from $1,000 to $10,000 per year. Neurosurgeons, anesthesiologists, orthopedic surgeons, foot far higher bills than general practitioners or psychiatrists. Urban physicians, especially in suit-prone areas like New York City or Los Angeles, pay much more than their small-town counterparts. Some higher-risk specialists in those large cities pay $20, 000 to $50,000 per year for their premiums: an amazing sum which is even more remarkable when one considers that fifteen years ago premiums ranged from $100 to $500 and almost never exceeded $1,000.

Many physicians cannot raise fees enough to afford these staggering rates. Insurance actuarial tables do not take into account the size or volume of the practice—only specialty and location. Moreover, premiums are due when a practice begins, long before patients have paid their bills. For an established practitioner this large out-of-pocket outlay may be feasible. However, consider the physician who is semi-retired; the academic physician who teaches extensively but wants to maintain a part-time practice, or the young specialist fresh out of his residency. Doctors have been driven out of practice, away from high-risk areas and into other fields of medicine because they couldn't support this staggering overhead. The high cost of malpractice protection threatens to rob cities like New York of critically needed specialists. It is frightening to think that medical services may be determined not by public need, but by the cost of insurance.

DEFENSIVE MEDICINE

"Defensive medicine" is a newcomer to our medical vocabulary. It implies the overordering of useless, nonindicated and sometimes risky tests to compile the most excruciatingly detailed patient record that covers every possible diagnosis in the event of a lawsuit.

How many times have you, a friend, or a relative gone to an emergency room with a minor bruise? In past years the physician would use a measure of diagnostic skill to help rule out a fracture. Now, concerned about his legal position, he will always order an X ray.

The same holds true for laboratory studies. Every hospitalized patient will, in many centers, have a complete battery of blood tests that may cost $100 or more. Perhaps 10 percent of those tests or even fewer are truly indicated.

"Defensive medicine" has been costly in a more insidious way. We saw earlier that the law requires a physician to practice medicine in accordance with the usual standards of his community: studies which should be performed must be; those which are not indicated can be excluded. Five years ago not ordering a particular X ray might have been reasonably acceptable by community standards—today it is not. "Defensive medicine" has changed the standards of medical practice and increased the physician's legal responsibilities.

MALPRACTICE SUITS—TWO POINTS OF VIEW

An argument frequently offered by proponents of continued malpractice litigation is that it keeps doctors on their toes and improves medical practice. The other side asserts that medical practice is impaired by the ever-present specter of a potential suit. Each side has some validity.

To some extent the alarm over malpractice suits and the paranoiac desire to avoid litigation has improved medical standards. Recently an attorney, arguing to the contrary, noted that people don't drive more carefully because they fear a potential lawsuit should they cause a collision. This is undoubtedly true, but it is an inappropriate analogy. The furthest thing from a motorist's mind is the possibility of a lawsuit, but malpractice suits are an ever-present threat very much in the mind and apt to guide the actions of a practicing physician. A relevant highway analogy would be the more common threat of a traffic ticket. Perhaps twenty years ago the rare malpractice suits were a distant threat. Today they are akin to traffic tickets, for they lurk behind each patient.

The same attorney argues that no physician wants to injure a patient. "Can the threat of a suit make him do any better than his innate drive to do the best he can?" Of course it can, and to believe otherwise is a naïve view of human nature. The desire to perform well is an important drive, but the necessity to do so adds an additional spark.

Even for the conscientious physician, shortcuts and careless practices may creep into his daily routine. Outside reminders provide an extra push and spawn additional safety measures. What about those physicians who don't care about their patients?—and there really are some. For them, the threat of a lawsuit may be their only reason for quality control.

Suit awareness has forced a critical evaluation of office and hospital practice. Numerous articles have appeared in medical periodicals advising physicians on how to make their practices "malpractice-proof." These recommendations, offered to protect physicians, more importantly protect patients, for they suggest safety precautions and the mending of trouble spots in daily practice.

Concerns about potential lawsuits have especially

affected hospital practice. Most hospitals have review committees whose vigor of surveillance and corrective powers have increased in recent years. Emergency room facilities, emergency procedures, nurses training, operating room activity, and intensive care have all improved. How many of these changes can be ascribed to fear of litigation and how many to innate conscientiousness, consumer pressures, and controls by hospital associations and accreditation boards is hard to weigh, but apprehension over potential suits undoubtedly plays some role.

Lawsuits themselves will also occasionally uncover trouble spots and generate beneficial changes. You can be sure that a hospital or a physician who is sued because of a particular error will make a special effort to minimize that kind of mistake in the future. If a patient falls out of bed because of a broken bedrail, breaks his hip, and successfully sues the hospital for $100,000, all of the hospital's bedrails will be checked the next day, and will continue to be checked at regular intervals. One might argue that the very fact of a patient's injury would stimulate such a safety check. Perhaps, but an incident that might be gradually forgotten will remain more vivid if it carries a $100,000 price tag.

Furthermore, there are many dangerous hospital and physician shortcuts which might never be uncovered if not brought to light by a lawsuit. Poor record keeping, an error in drug administration, unsanitary food-handling practices, may go unnoticed until they are revealed in court.

This does not mean that malpractice litigation is a good way to control the quality of hospital and medical care. Just as the ideal solution to crime is not to imprison, but rather to abolish poverty, enhance personal and social morality, and stimulate social cohesion and purpose, the best way to end malpractice is through voluntary internal controls such as review committees, rigorous licensing procedures, mandatory physician reexaminations, and individual commitment to care and diligence.

Although malpractice litigation has accomplished some good, in most respects it has been damaging. Its effect on cost and distribution of medical care have been discussed. Additionally, it has destroyed physician morale and devastated what remained of the doctor-patient relationship, and threatens to generate backlash litigation which may deprive deserving claimants of their just awards.

Doctors and patients have become legal adversaries while they are waging a joint battle against the same illness. This paradox has seriously affected the success of medical care. One can ask, "Does it really matter whether the doctor and his patient trust each other? Do the bacteria that are being treated with the penicillin know the difference?" The bacteria may not know or care, but the doctor-patient relationship is an essential feature of successful medical practice.

All illnesses are complex. Their courses are determined by the disease itself and by the patient's emotional response to that disease. The contribution that personal, ill-defined factors make to an illness is highly variable, depending upon the personality of the patient, his psychological makeup, environmental pressures, and other subconscious motivations. A family man on an hourly wage may brush aside a cold. His child, anxious to have a school vacation, may be bedridden for three days with the very same virus. In most cases, psychological factors like these are so important that they, rather than the amount of infection or the location of the fracture, play a major role in recovery. Although the emotional makeup of the patient most strongly determines this feature of healing, the doctor can and must play an important modifying role.

Any technically competent practitioner can give penicillin for a Strep throat or properly cast a simple fracture, but the intangible emotional support a doctor can provide necessitates that the patient feel the doctor is doing the best he can and that he is in capable hands, or the illness may drag on. To convey this essential air of concern and competence the physician must truly want to help his patient. In a climate of anxiety and distrust that critical area of patient care withers.

Getting well also requires more than the doctor doing his job—the patient must do his. He must follow the doctor's orders, take medication at the right time in the right way, restrict activities as necessary, and eat the recommended diet. These tangibles are crucial to the patient's recovery, but they will not be adhered to unless the patient believes in his doctor's ability and trusts his judgment. Postoperative patients, particularly, demand the strongest emotional support. The rate at which they get up and out after an operation depends on their innate drives, which may be substantially modified by the attending surgeon. One patient, certain that his surgeon cured him and pushed by the doctor's solicitous encouragement, will recuperate quickly. His roommate, rarely visited by his surgeon and uncertain of his competency, may languish for weeks.

By damaging the doctor-patient rapport malpractice litigation has undermined this much-needed emotional support, which has prolonged recovery times and encouraged disability. An actual lawsuit can promote disability in another way. The patient with pressing responsibilities may recover quickly. A second individual with the very same problem and a lawsuit in progress may not. This may not be a conscious effort on his part, but the dream of future awards can be a strong subconscious motivation for continued disability. Therefore, at the same time as it attempts to compensate for an injury, malpractice litigation can prolong that injury.

Unfortunately, unbridled malpractice litigation has spawned a violent backlash from insurance companies and physician organizations, as well as many proposals for alternative solutions. Some of those alternatives, which will be discussed in the next chapter, are being vigorously promoted without careful examination. The premature passage of poorly studied, unfair, or unworkable legislation could deprive deserving plaintiffs of just settlements.

Most arguments supporting or decrying the present system of dealing with medical malpractice miss the mark: the fundamental issue is not whether malpractice suits are good or bad, but how malpractice can be reduced and the rights of both patients and doctors protected.

Proper solutions will take mutual effort and agreement. First, medical practice must be improved so that malpractice injuries are minimized. Second, the runaway costs of litigation, insurance, and defensive medicine must be checked. Finally, the rights of those who are truly victims of malpractice must be protected. The solutions to those compelling problems will benefit all concerned—the doctors, the patients, and the insurers.

11

Solutions

Until recently the medical community and society enjoyed a cooperative relationship. Each made minor adjustments and compromises, and changes evolved gradually. In the past few years, however, slow evolution has been replaced by confrontation, distrust, and anger.

An analogy can be drawn between the changing doctor-patient relationship and a crumbling marriage. At the start of their lives together the husband and wife had occupied narrowly circumscribed, conventional roles: the man dominated and the woman submitted unquestioningly. But the wife, with good reason, began to feel that she was trapped, unproductive, and ineffectual. At the age of forty she rebelled, demanding freedom and the opportunity to pursue a career. Failing to sway her traditional husband, she filed for divorce.

Similarly, physicians and the American people are on the brink of divorce. They have lost confidence in each other's motives and integrity. Just as divorce is the final sign of a failing marriage, so is litigation the last resort for the frustrated patient.

Reversing the doctor-patient crisis demands an attack on problems such as physician carelessness and thoughtlessness. An effective program must, additionally, confront the litigation crisis and offer new alternatives. The basis for malpractice injuries, the rapport between doctors and patients, and the runaway costs of malpractice insurance must be dealt with simultaneously. It is essential to find solutions which respect the rights of physicians but at the same time guarantee the patient legal protection.

Most remedial suggestions fall into the following categories: internal improvements in medical practice overseen by the medical community itself; tighter governmental control of the distribution and quality of medical care; changes in the financing of malpractice insurance; changes in the payment of malpractice compensation, and alterations in the current system of litigation.

MALPRACTICE ALTERNATIVES— THE QUALITY OF MEDICAL CARE

Punishing errant physicians and rewarding injured patients are necessary functions of our legal system, but their powers as deterrents are limited. What, then, can be done to end malpractice? There are two fundamental problems, closely intertwined but with different solutions: the problem of careless medicine, which is the root of negligent injuries; and society's attitude toward physicians, which is the major stimulus for most malpractice suits.

Many of the common errors leading to patient injuries have been discussed—being unavailable when needed, failing to request specialized assistance or order necessary tests, improperly monitoring patients, and entrusting subordinates with too much responsibility. These frequent pitfalls in daily practice demand change. Medicine is an essential public service with no competitive pressures. Doctors, no matter how good or bad, how careful or careless, are always busy. Any profession in such constant demand can fall victim to complacency.

To practice medicine one needs to attend an accredited medical school, spend one year as an intern (not required in a number of states), and pass a written examination. Almost all American medical school graduates do pass and, for $50 or $100, can obtain a license in almost any state. Thereafter the licensed physician is free to practice medicine with no reevaluation for the rest of his career. Moreover, he can, within the legal bounds of his licensure, practice any aspect of medicine and surgery. He could perform brain operations or put in heart valves, although no one without specialized training would undertake such delicate cases. The point, however, is that the law sanctions the physician's involvement in areas far beyond his level of expertise. Until recently surveillance of doctors was nonexistent, and the revoking of a medical license was a newsworthy event. Physicians lost their licenses only for major transgressions such as drug addiction or a felony conviction.

Partly as a result of the malpractice crisis and partly because of consumer pressures, the medical societies and licensing bureaus are slowly but surely changing their policies: specialists must take rigorous certification examinations, and postgraduate review courses have been organized. Some hospitals require their staff physicians to take periodic refresher courses. Specialty recertification exams are being instituted and, for the first time, some incompetent physicians are losing their hospital privileges and medical licenses. Admittedly, all of these changes are long overdue and are progressing very slowly, but they indicate a desire in the medical community to clean house and improve the standards of medical care.

This internal monitoring is being supplemented by federal programs. One plan is exemplary as an attempt to control the standards of medical practice. The Professional Standards Review Organization (PSRO) was established by Congress in 1972. It provides that local medical societies, or the federal government if necessary, establish guidelines for the diagnosis and treatment of diseases, with review committees to oversee proper implementation. The AMA argues that bureaucratic standardization is an unwise intrusion into patient care and that computerized recipes will be unworkable and ultimately dangerous for the patient. After all, the AMA maintains, it is the responsible physician who can observe moment-to-moment changes and take immediate, appropriate action, and he must not be shackled by a system of rote directions.

It is true that there are serious dangers inherent in a system of standardized directions for diagnosis and treatment. There must be a built-in flexibility that permits frequent modifications in response to individual patient needs. If such flexibility is maintained, however, the PSRO may provide an important watchdog function. Their reviewing role will ensure physician accountability and will uncover major and repetitive deviations from usual standard management. Regardless of its final place in the health care system, the PSRO bill reflects the federal government's concern about the quality of medical care.

Such bills, stricter licensure requirements, regular reexaminations, and medical society surveillance and censure are all designed to improve medical care and reduce patient risk. These should decrease the incidence of medical malpractice, but an additional control is needed to slow runaway litigation.

We have seen that the desire to sue motivates more lawsuits than do specific transgressions. If physicians hope to reduce the number of claims against them, they must wage a concerted campaign to combat adverse public opinion. There are lawsuit-prone doctors who are frequent defendants. Some of them are repeatedly guilty of malpractice. Many, however, are victims of their personalities. Their hostile and arrogant manner infuriates patients and engenders a desire to sue with the slightest provocation.

Some degree of patient alienation is unavoidable. The busy schedules of today's practitioners, the end of the family physician, and the brief contacts with the specialist undermine patient confidence. But the physician can make a conscious effort to be approachable and concerned. He can attempt to answer his patient's questions, to involve him in the therapeutic plan, and to strive to gain his respect.

There are those who argue that it is futile to try to teach an adult how to deal with people. If he has not learned effective interaction skills during his formative years, the reasoning goes, he never will. This is not entirely true. The practice of medicine, with its constant exposure to death and sickness, can be dehumanizing and emotionally debilitating. In order to handle the anguish of patient suffering, physicians must become detached. As a defensive reaction they begin to forget that they are dealing with human patients rather than with abstract diseases. Some of this process of dehumanization can be reversed through active reemphasis of medicine's humanitarian goals and of the psychological and emotional impact of disease. An increased self-awareness may help the physician interact more personally with his patients and their illnesses. Patients, sensing an empathetic response, may regain some confidence in their doctors, thus losing the vengeful desire to sue.

MALPRACTICE ALTERNATIVES—FINANCING AND LITIGATION

In the next few years there will be substantial changes in the financing of malpractice insurance and possibly in the litigation of suits. As is so often the case, many of the recommended changes arising from the present atmosphere of crisis are unworkable and potentially disastrous.

A barrage of suggestions from medical societies, insurance companies, attorneys' organizations, and legislative bodies has been urged on the community. Several bills are before the Congress, and almost every state legislature is considering some aspect of the malpractice problem. Recommendations range from suggestions by outraged physicians that all legal redress for medical injuries be outlawed to arbitration and no-fault programs so diluted by exceptions and options that they offer no hope for meaningful change. The reasons for these varied and conflicting proposals are obvious: people are troubled by the developments in medical malpractice, but no one has a single best solution to offer. Moreover, it is virtually impossible to distinguish worthwhile and well-intentioned alternatives from self-serving ones.

The public must protect its interests by participating in

these important legislative decisions. To do so, patients and potential claimants must be familiar with current proposals. Some of these—specifically those dealing with the financing of malpractice insurance—will affect the public pocketbook. Those dealing with proposed changes in methods of litigation will have other, more far-reaching ramifications. The majority of recommendations fall into two general categories: changes in malpractice insurance methods and changes in the litigation process.

CHANGES IN INSURANCE PRACTICES

The insurance system may be altered through new methods of financing, by changes in payment eligibility, or by both. Unless a new litigation system eliminates insurance requirements, doctors must remain insured. The practice of medicine and the distribution of practicing physicians cannot be jeopardized by the inability to obtain insurance or to pay the staggering premiums. One frequently advocated solution is to have the federal or state goverment bear part of the insurance burden. Since medicine is such a critical public service, the consumer nay have to finance some of these costs directly, as with other goverment-subsidized health care programs such as Medicare, Medicaid, and the inevitable National Health Insurance measure.

Another alternative under active scrutiny is to have insurance companies pool their resources. Such an action would keep the insurance burden in the private sector but would spread the risks among all of the carriers.

A final alternative may be to increase medical society and physician self-insurance. Under such a system the medical society or group of physicians, rather than a commercial company, would become the insurer. Physician contributors would provide the working capital for routine claims; coverage for any very large claims would be provided by another company or by the federal government.

This type of system, which is under active consideration, has several advantages. Because the company owners would be physicians they would be in an ideal position to police their members actively and accurately. They could screen applicants for competency and evidence of insurance risk. They could oversee the practices of their members to minimize future risk. Finally, they could review any claims themselves and settle, if appropriate, or prepare a defense, if necessary, far more cheaply than a large, general insurance company.

An amusing but quite serious suggestion was offered in a recent letter to the editor of a medical journal. A physician, frustrated with the malpractice system, proposed a type of self-insurance to be purchased by the patient. On entering the hospital the patient would voluntarily buy a malpractice insurance policy—a particular operation would require a ten- or twenty-dollar policy that would insure the individual against negligence.

The author of the proposal incorrectly compared the idea to flight insurance. The airline passenger is not protecting himself against negligence; he is taking out a life insurance policy. If a crash occurs he or his family could sue the airline company for negligence. Similarly, the patient has the constitutional right to sue if he is the victim of medical negligence.

In addition to proposed changes in insurance financing, there have been suggestions for alternatives to current compensation eligibility. These could affect the physician's eligibility for malpractice compensation. At the present time most policies cover the physician for any incidents which occurred while he was insured, regardless of his current insurance status. Under these "occurrence policies" a physician who has left practice, retired, changed companies, or lost his insurance remains protected against suits resulting from events that took place while he was insured by a particular company. Such protection is important to shield the physician from liability for claims based on long-past actions.

Some insurance companies are advocating, as an alternative to the occurrence policy, a "claims-made" program, whereby a doctor is covered only during the time he is carrying insurance with a particular company. If he retires or drops his insurance for any reason, any claim made against him for an earlier incident will not be backed, despite the fact that he was insured when the incident occurred.

Insurance companies point to several economic necessities for this revised coverage. Many claims are made years after the alleged negligence took place. Moreover, once a suit is filed, it may take years to complete the litigation process. The delay places insurance companies in an unusually vulnerable position, since they cannot base their financial planning on normal actuarial methods and formulate premium rates accordingly. Malpractice insurance is particularly affected by such a delayed and unanticipated claim policy, because of the very nature of malpractice injuries, which may not be evident for many years.

In most states there are statutes of limitations of one to five years to limit the time that can elapse between an injury and a suit. These statutes have been modified by the "discovery rule." According to this rule, which the insurance companies have heatedly opposed, the statute of limitations begins not at the time that the incident occurred, but at the point when the act of negligence could have first been discovered. The discovery rule has been abused by some attorneys attempting to litigate expired cases, but the principle often has a valid basis. For example, the victim of surgical negligence in whose abdomen a sponge was left after a routine operation may not develop any complications until two years later. There would have been no way for the patient to have recognized the negligent act earlier. To eliminate his right to sue would be grossly unfair. A similar example is the patient whose cancer was misdiagnosed and not caught until two or three years later. A double outrage would result if an individual were first victimized by a medical error and were then unable to pursue legal recourse.

The above two examples illustrate the rationale behind the discovery rule. However, there must be a way to curtail its abuses, which have become all too common. The rule should be applied only in cases where the patient can substantiate an act of negligence which went undetected for a period of time.

Although the claims-made policies would not alter the discovery rule or shorten protracted court battles, they would determine that companies are protecting those only who are currently holding premiums rather than those who were clients twenty years ago. Such a program would enable an insurance company to predict its expenditures more accurately.

Medical societies and physicians who are aware of the proposed claims-made change are aghast. They feel that it will increase their individual risk and will make many physicians personally vulnerable to large financial losses even after retirement. These fears are realistic. Either the medical societies themselves may have to pick up those claims not covered under the claims-made system, or the company will have to keep a physician on its books—for instance, after his retirement—for a small annual premium.

Most Americans are familiar with no-fault insurance as it applies to the center of the malpractice arena. There have been a number of bills introduced in Congress and state legislatures which, because of their various modifications, exceptions, and options, are not true no-fault bills.

A true no-fault program implies that any unexpected injury deserves compenstaion without regard to fault or liability. In other words, *every* patient who developed any complication—from a minor pain to the loss of life—would be eligible for compensation. Whether or not the complication resulted from medical negligence, the patient would receive some financial recompense.

Supporters of no-fault measures point to Workman's Compensation as their model. To the extent that Workman's Compensation grants all covered employees a certain amount for injury or disability and eliminates their right to sue the employer, it is a no-fault system. However, the analogy extends no further. First, there are a definite number of job-related disabilities; for example, a worker can lose a limb, be blinded, or die. Workman's Compensation clearly defines financial losses in terms of lost income and medical expenses. Consequently it is possible to establish actuarial tables, which enable boards to review cases of injury and rule on their validity. Secondly, since most accidents occur by chance and not as the result of employer negligence, litigation would go against the majority of workers.

No-fault malpractice insurance bears little resemblance to Workman's Compensation. Whereas work-related injuries can usually be attributed to a specific accident, medical complications involve a vast number of variables—the duration of the illness, the types of associated problems, the quality of care, the individual response to drugs and other therapy.

Consider, for instance, the healthy young woman who dies from an unforeseen complication after a gallbladder operation. Can she be compared to the severely ill diabetic patient of exactly the same age who died the same way? Or the man who is blind in one eye. Is his loss of the remaining eye the same as the loss of one eye in a previously normal man? And what of the two patients who require ulcer operations? One needs an emergency procedure to arrest vigorous bleeding; the other's operation is elective. If they die postoperatively, should both cases be awarded equal compensation? In one instance the procedure was potentially life-saving; in the other it was not. These cases illustrate the enormous complexity of the medical malpractice problem. Determining the relative or absolute values of medical injuries is a staggering task, approaching the impossible.

Unlike work-related injuries, medical complications are often not readily definable. If a surgeon makes a gross error or a drug causes a serious reaction the complication is obvious; but the majority of medical occurrences are not so clear-cut and could as easily result from the natural course of a disease or variations in the normal healing process as from a definable medical complication. For example, one person's cut might heal in four days, while another's, in the same place, might take two weeks. Clearly, the longer healing period would not be a complication, but rather an individual difference. However, if the same situation is applied to the hospitalized patient convalescing from an operation, the definition of a complication becomes more complex. Consider the following illustration.

Two healthy young men, each of whom had undergone similar hernia repair operations, shared a room in the hospital. One was discharged in one week, the other in three. The second man assumed that his protracted stay resulted from a complication, whereas actually it was due to the preference of his surgeon, who routinely kept his patients in the hospital for that length of time.

But other factors might also have made the prolonged hospitalization necessary. There might have been a naturally slower rate of healing, a slightly larger hernia with a more extensive operation, a different type of surgical repair. Or there might have been a true complication—excessive bleeding with blood-clot formation, infection, accidental tearing of the healing tissues. It is obvious, then, that even in such a seemingly straightforward case, defining a complication is a monumental task. In patients with profound illnesses or several concomitant problems, the difficulty becomes even greater.

Individual differences, both psychological and physical, further complicate the picture. Such factors are particularly important when the patient must actively and vigorously participate in his recovery. One patient may walk within a week after a hip replacement; another may require a month; a third may never get back on his feet. These different responses may result from a specific complication or from such individual qualities as personal fortitude, motivation, and determination. To separate a physical complication from a personal reaction may be impossible.

The foregoing examples highlight the difficulties in interpreting complications. A no-fault insurance system would subject almost every illness to review, and the number of administrators required to oversee this operation would be staggering. A program which proposes to reward any and all complications is doomed to failure because, as we have seen, in the majority of cases it is impossible even to define a complication.

Although it is no less complex to evaluate complications under the present jury system, there are far fewer cases to consider. Only those complications which resulted from alleged physician negligence come to the attention of the courts. Under the no-fault system the fundamental question would be: Was the medical problem a complication or simply an individual response to treatment? Under the present system, on the other hand, the issue is: Is there evidence of physician negligence? This question can be difficult to answer, but it is much easier to document physician causation through factual evidence and expert testimony than it is to distinguish between individual responses and complications.

The ill-defined nature of a complication, then, makes no-fault an unworkable system. Moreover, it would produce administrative and economic chaos. In no-fault every "complication" would be claimable regardless of negligence, and the number of claims would thereby be multiplied by thousands, or perhaps hundreds of thousands. Pain after an injection, a drug rash, a minor wound infection, a fainting spell from a medication, bleeding after childbirth necessitating a hysterectomy, a prolonged sinus infection resisting antibiotic treatment—all could be construed as complications requiring the processing of a claim which could lead to a financial award. Thousands of claims adjusters and a monstrous bureaucratic network would be needed to handle the load. The public cost would be staggering. Management costs compounded by claims awards would far exceed our current malpractice outlay.

CHANGES IN LITIGATION

The Constitution protects the right to pursue a civil case in a court of one's peers, but questions have recently been raised about the role of the courts in malpractice suits.

Malpractice cases differ from other civil tort problems in a number of ways. To begin with, the issues involved are highly technical, and often even a well-instructed jury cannot fully grasp the problems. Secondly, emotional and subjective elements play a much greater role in malpractice than in other types of negligence. One need only look at the verdict that is awarded against a doctor whose negligence caused the loss of an extremity, and compare it with the award for the same injury resulting from an auto accident caused by a reckless driver. The accident victim may get $30,000, while the patient gets $500,000. Emotional bias against physicians has turned the tide toward large verdicts—members of a jury view the doctor as a common adversary. Thirdly, the cost of malpractice litigation is so high that the usual court processes are bankrupting the insurance companies and straining the American health care budget. Finally, the wave of suits against doctors is so dangerous to the public welfare that unusual controls must be exercised to protect the public interest.

The foregoing factors point up the differences between

medical malpractice and other types of negligence and justify the proposed changes in the malpractice system. There are two fundamental problems which a revised program of malpractice litigation should aim to alleviate: the increase in minor, often groundless claims, and the escalation of award amounts in high-value cases.

The practice of settling claims was touched upon earlier. A dollars-and-cents illustration will make the rationale clearer: In a recent case a young woman died from what the family's attorneys felt was a drug reaction. They filed suit against four physicians, two hospitals, and two drug companies. Four physicians and a pharmacologist reviewed the case for the defense and found it to be unequivocally without merit. The woman's death had actually resulted from a fall and was unrelated to the taking of any drugs.

The five attorneys and five medical experts were compensated at the rate of $50 to $200 per hour. Most had come from distant areas, and they spent two days reviewing the case and its defense. Their total bill came to $50,000. Two weeks before the trial the insurance companies awarded the claimant $15,000. It was a great deal of money for a groundless claim, but trial would have cost an additional $40,000, which the companies refused to expend.

Nearly 10,000 such nonmeritorious claims are filed annually; 6,000 may be dropped with no award, but even those necessitate costly preparation. The others are settled, like the one described above, for an amount far greater than their true worth but considerably less than trial costs.

For every valid claim five are lodged because of dissatisfaction with the physician or frustration over a chronic disability, or simply because the patient feels—and rightly so—that the insurance companies may give him something for nothing. This practice is encouraged by the insurance companies themselves, who do reward invalid claims, and by some attorneys who exploit the system. Even ethical attorneys wanting to accept only valid cases contribute to these financial problems by failing to call in competent medical consultants to screen cases before filing suit.

The medical community, too, has contributed to the deluge of invalid lawsuits. Until recently physicians recoiled at the word "malpractice" and refused to cooperate with the legal community, thereby leaving the lawyers without competent consultants to help them evaluate the real merits of a case.

Although each interest group is equally to blame for the avalanche of nonmeritorious claims, none will admit to its own role in contributing to the dilemma. The lawyers blame negligent doctors for the increase in suits, and also complain that they cannot get competent medical counsel. The doctors maintain that the fault lies with the greedy lawyers, whose excessive contingency fees make them professional parasites. Neither group feels kindly toward the insurance companies, who have been unwilling to participate in finding new solutions.

At last, however, doctors and lawyers are beginning to recognize their common problems and to realize that the malpractice issue is of major national concern. Public outrage and proposed legislative rearrangements have prompted negotiations between the two professional camps. The result has been a vast number of suggested alternatives to the current system, many of which hold the promise for truly effective change.

LAWYERS' FEES

A source of bitter strife between physicians and plaintiff attorneys arises over legal fees. Negligence work in general is handled by lawyers on a contingency basis. The attorney receives a certain percentage, usually 30 to 50 percent of the total award.

Plaintiff attorneys argue that this practice is justified and necessary. They claim that contingency arrangements enable economically deprived clients to enjoy legal protection, for it would be a rare individual who could afford to advance legal fees at $50 to $100 per hour. Contingency fees defer the payment until the trial is over, and the lawyer gets nothing if the case fails.

Plaintiff attorneys assert that the risks of getting nothing if they lose the case justify the great compensation for a victory. They point to statistics which show that plaintiff attorneys make almost the same amount per hour as defense lawyers who are paid on an hourly basis. Finally, they maintain that the contingency fee is beneficial to the medical-legal process, by providing an incentive to weed out bad claims. Because the attorney stands to lose time and money if the case fails to bring an award, he is less likely to accept a groundless case.

Although there are some elements of truth to these arguments, critics have effectively countered them. Opponents of contingency payment point out that a plaintiff attorney concerned about the ability of the poor client to bring a case to court could defer the payment of an hourly fee until the end of the trial. Thus, the indigent client could still prosecute his claim, and the lawyer would receive his fees at the end, just as in contingency cases. The only difference would be that the dollar amount would reflect the number of hours the attorney had worked rather than the generosity of the jury. If the case lost, the lawyer could still relinquish his fee as he does in a losing contingency case. Thus the poor client remains protected.

It may have been true in the past that contingency fees discouraged frivolous cases, but today they are not effective deterrents against groundless suits. Insurance companies will give small payoffs even to a very weak case. As a result, a plaintiff attorney can put almost no time into a case (he may have only to draft a complaint and file suit) in order to get a settlement. Moreover, experience has shown that cases which do go to trial are usually decided in favor of the doctor. This suggests that lawyers are accepting a large number of nonmeritorious cases.

Even if the contingency-fee basis were to discourage low-value nuisance suits (and, as we have seen, they probably do not), they would encourage high-value ones. A case may have little merit, but if it is potentially worth $2 million it is fertile territory for a plaintiff attorney. Thus the current contingency arrangement ecourages the pursuit of cases that may be weakly founded but that have high potential awards.

It is true that contingency fees may make the attorney work harder for his client. This may be the only firm justification for a system which, because of its abuse and potential dangers, requires reform. The best suggestion is a sliding contingency scale such as the one practiced in New Jersey, where the percentage decreases as the recovery increases. Thus the lawyer might get 40 percent of the first $20,000 but only 10 percent of any amount over $100,000.

This system alleviates the most serious abuse of the contingency plan—the pushing of high-value, low-merit cases. With the sliding scale the attorney has no such financial incentive.

CHANGES IN LITIGATION

A number of medical societies, hospitals, and physicians have recommended that patients be forced to sign disclaimers of liability, or guarantees that they will not sue in case of injury. Physicians warn that in view of the current malpractice crisis they may soon be compelled to accept only patients who have signed such forms.

While the doctors' despair is understandable, contracts of this type are not legally binding. The unfairness of a contract which denies the right to litigation is especially obvious in the case of a patient signing under duress. Several cases have already proven that physicians can be sued despite carefully worded waivers of liability.

Another extreme possibilty which some physicians have suggested would be for a doctor to sign all of his personal possessions over to his spouse, carry no malpractice insurance, and thereby become judgment-proof. Several physicians who carried out this plan found that they were, indeed, protected from their patients, but they were at the mercy of their husbands or wives. When their spouses took off and left them with nothing, the doctors had no legal recourse. A physician considering this drastic measure must, first, live in a state where it is legal to have no personal possessions and, second, trust his spouse more than his patients. Actually, the rate of divorce among doctors is far higher than the rate of malpractice suits!

It is time to abandon such unrealistic propositions and get down to the serious planning of corrective measures. Some of the proposed measures do contain the potential for success. Although all have some features to recommend them, deliberation and caution must prevail before any of the proposals is legislated. If they are not carefully tested and evaluated, chaotic struggles will ensue, individuals will be deprived of their fundamental rights, and the problem will be even more complicated than it is now.

SCREENING PANELS AND MEDIATION AND ARBITRATION BOARDS

In order to treat the problem of proliferating nonmeritorious claims a preliminary screening of malpractice cases will become a necessity. Many review systems have been proposed, and several have been put into practice, including public and private screening panels, review committees, and arbitration boards. All aim to weed out frivolous claims. lessen jury bias, and assure that cases are screened and, in some cases, ruled upon by competent reviewers who have the technical backgrounds to grasp the issues. Careful screening will reduce costs, decrease the number of cases that the courts must see, and increase the chances for fair decisions. The format, as well as the power, of these panels and boards varies; some contain more promise than others, but all rest on sound concepts in the best interest of the public.

Defendants and their insurers advocate the use of medical screening panels, composed entirely of physicians who review the case and recommend settlement or legal defense.

Often the panels supply medical experts to defend cases that have no merit. The overall value of this sytem is limited, since plaintiffs and their attorneys would not put their trust in the decision of an all-doctor screening panel.

A solution more satisfactory to both parties is the joint screening panel, which is composed of a fairer cross section—physicians, attorneys, and sometimes clergymen or other members of the community. In Pima County, Arizona, such a panel had proven exemplary. Both plaintiff and defense have uniformly accepted the decisions of the panel, and since its establishment very few cases against physicians have been prosecuted. Negligence cases have been settled out of court, and groundless ones have been dropped.

Although proponents of the joint screening panel have pointed to Pima County as a model, several factors make the experience there unique. It is a small community, where the bar and the medical societies have strong sanction powers, and public opinion is very important. Moreover, the community, by virtue of its closeness, has better doctor-patient relations.

In larger metropolitan areas joint screening panels have met with less success. Although the panels include lawyers, plaintiff attorneys are often distrustful of the system. They argue that the physicians are strongly biased and can use their medical expertise to sway the opinions of the other panelists. The use of such panels is always voluntary and their value becomes limited when poor legal and public acceptance makes plaintiffs unwilling to abide by their decisions.

Some panels have extended their powers by supplying experts to the plaintiff if they find in his favor; by making their decisions public or available in court if neither side is willing to compromise; by insisting that the plaintiff attorney turn the case over to another lawyer should the plaintiff ignore an adverse decision and decide to sue. These measures act as controls on plaintiff attorneys, who might otherwise use the panels as a source of medical information on the case without intending to follow their recommendations.

Despite such additonal powers the screening panels continue to face the problem of public acceptance. There are two solutions: to use private screening panels composed of physicians hired to review a case; and to form, by statute, mandatory screening panels or arbitration boards which would leave the prospective claimant no alternative but to accept the final decision.

Private screening panels, a number of which are currently in operation, offer a significant advantage to the public. They eliminate bias against the individual client, who can be either defendant or plaintiff, because they are hired by him. Although such panels are composed of physicians who can effectively review the issues, the panelists are prepared to support the client if the facts are in his favor. The panel may recommend settlement to an insurance company or help the client to locate and prepare experts for trial if settlement is not reached. It has advantages over an appointed public panel, because it works for the client, who is thus more willing to accept its final decision. A number of such organizations are operating successfully around the country.

Publicly appointed panels may become necessary if the malpractice crisis continues to mushroom. There are several disadvantages to such panels. It would be costly to review all malpractice cases, and the usual problems of public bureaucracies would slow down the process. The panels would have to be selected with great care in order to preserve the rights of the citizen and win the confidence of the legal and medical communities and the public.

None of the screening panels would totally replace the court system, because they would make recommendations which could be rejected. They might have certain powers of control, as described above, but they could not deny the constitutional right to trial by jury. Panels would simply reduce the number of cases, particularly nonmeritorious ones.

Binding arbitration is another alternative, which *would* eliminate court litigation. The public should be wary of this solution, since it would rob it of its right to due process. Binding arbitration would require both parties to submit their dispute to a board, which would review the issues and make a decision about merit and dollar value. The decision might be subject to appeal, if such a provision were predetermined, but there could be no court action. In certain cases binding arbitration might be practical—for small claims of less than $5,000 or $10,000, for instance. Out-of-court settlement of such claims would substantially reduce current malpractice costs. A possible solution, then, would be to use binding arbitration to settle small-value claims, while reserving court trials for high-value claims.

Another important step should be the establishment of upper limits for specific injuries. The figures should be flexible enough to reflect economic changes and actual financial losses. In other words, lost income of the principal wage earner should result in compensation for the family and the payment of all rehabilitation costs; on the other hand, punitive damages and pain and suffering should receive payment according to established, finite values. At present a host of variables, such as the feelings of a specific jury and the competency of the attorneys on either side, determine the awards for these types of injuries. A plaintiff might recover $100,000 or $1 million for a particular injury, depending on the jury and the trial lawyer. Such an artificial system of awards is unfair to the American consumer, who must ultimately bear the financial burden.

Let us consider an example of a revised system. Assume that the injured plaintiff is a child negligently blinded shortly after birth. The verdict for the child should include all of the expenses of special education, possibly an amount for loss of income, and a fixed sum for pain and suffering. The verdict would reflect actual financial losses plus a preset amount for suffering. The reward would, in this case, be high, but at least it would be possible to determine the exact value of the case, whereas under the present system there would be a $2 million margin of uncertainty, depending on the whims of jury sympathy and attorney appeal.

12

Patient's Rights, Doctor's Rights

Although doctor and patient share a common objective—to cure an illness—their approaches and concerns are often at odds. The patient's disease or injury is a threat to his well-being or even his life. He can hardly view it dispassionately. The doctor, on the other hand, if he is to help effectively, must be objective. He cannot afford to have his analytical thinking clouded by emotional involvement. This major difference in orientation—on one side emotional, on the other detached—is a fundamental source of doctor-patient strife.

Another clash arises because doctors often fail to provide the treatment that the patient expects. The average patient knows far less about medicine than the physician whom he consults, but he often has certain expectations about treatment. He may expect a cure for the cold, an X ray for the arm injury, sutures for the hand laceration, a brace for the painful back, binders for the contused ribs, or an antibiotic for the sore throat. Often the doctor, after reaching a medically sound conclusion, must deviate from those expectations. It may be a monumental task indeed for the physician to convince his patient that his way is best. He will be able to do so only if he can instill respect and confidence and if he can convincingly explain his recommendations.

The patient's problem and his expectations for treatment and cure are major concerns to him, and he may reasonably expect his physician to approach those concerns with sympathetic understanding. If he does not, he has denied his patient a basic necessity of good medical care.

The patient may want assurance that he has merely a cold and not pneumonia. Or he may realize that he has a cold, but may hope for curative treatment. The physican may respond to this patient in two ways: by recognizing the concern or hope and reacting sympathetically, or by evidencing displeasure at being bothered by these trivial, untreatable illnesses. In the first case, the patients' rights have been respected. He will respond favorably—not cured but reassured. In the second, his rights have been violated. He will feel wronged, probably mistreated, and will find another doctor.

Similarly, parents may bring a child to the physician demanding an X ray of an injured arm. That decision is a medical one which can only be made by the doctor. The doctor may resent the family's demand and be obviously annoyed at their presumption, or he may recognize their concern, accept their lack of medical sophistication, and reassuringly demonstrate that the physical findings alone rule out any possibility of a fracture.

The man who hurts his ribs may remember his childhood days when these injuries were routinely treated with chest binders. He is unaware of the fact that these have recently fallen into disfavor since their restrictive action can lead to pulmonary complications, such as pneumonia. The patient has a right to expect a careful and considerate explanation of why his preconceived expectations for treatment are not being met.

The ability to be understanding, reassuring, and perceptive of patients' concerns is not shared equally by all physicians. It is a part of the art of medicine discussed earlier. To some extent this ability is a natural talent, but it can be improved with practice and attention. The physician who denies the patient his right to courteous consideration is a ripe target for lawsuits.

The patient who is treated fairly owes certain responsibilities to the doctor. The patient must not be so committed to his preconceived assessment that he is unwilling to accept a contrary medical opinion if it is carefully formulated and basically sensible. If the physician explains that the arm is not broken and an X ray is unnecessary, that antibiotics are not used for colds, that chest binders can be dangerous, that the small laceration in the child's arm can be treated with tape closures rather than with sutures, the patient should concede that his own judgement is probably less accurate than the physician's.

In addition to courtesies and sensitivity, the patient has the right to expect conscientious care from his doctor. He deserves the highest quality, most competent help his community can provide. The doctor may not be able to offer any help, but it must not be because he failed to be thorough. The disease may kill the patient; the doctor must not.

The doctor in turn justifiably expects patient cooperation. His patient must abide by recommendations of reduced activity, special diets, reduction of stress. He must take the prescribed medications as ordered and must report any sign of an abnormal reaction or a therapeutic failure. The doctor has the right to anticipate this level of patient cooperation, without which the best treatment will inevitably fail.

Those rights form the basis of the doctor-patient relationship. When they are violated and the relationship breaks down, the legal forum is resorted to. Here, too, patients and doctors have basic rights. The patient has the right to legal redress for unnecessary injuries. The doctor has the responsibility to pay for his mistakes, but the right to be shielded from unfair harassment. Recent confrontations between the public and American physicians have raised a question of fundamental social significance: whether medical practitioners are somehow special and different from any other occupational group. The answer will determine what happens to malpractice litigation in the future and, more importantly, may set unusual precedents for favoritism towards one group.

Apologists for medical malpractice ask, "How can society punish a physician for making an 'honest' mistake?" The term "honest" implies lack of premeditation, an accident. It asks that our judical system not only assess negligence and its consequences, but that it also judge the doctor's intent.

No doctor wants to make a serious mistake, nor does any other citizen guilty of negligence. A careless driver does not intend to kill an elderly pedestrian; an inept contractor does not plan to have the wall of the building collapse; the conscientious engineer does not want the subway train to derail and hit a wall; the hapless crane operator does not want his crane to come crashing down crushing five parked cars. Yet all of these "honest" mistakes occurred nonetheless. Honest or not, intentional or not, the person responsible was legally accountable, and either he or his employer was personally liable for damages.

Even a physician highly critical of our current malpractice system would not forgive these "honest mistakes" if his mother were the victim of the reckless driver, if he were caught in the collapsed building or the train crash, or if his car were destroyed by the crane. By asking that physicians be immune from legal prosecution he has established a dual standard: one for himself as a defendant, another as victim of someone else's negligence.

This double standard is most dramatically emphasized by the observation that physicians sue other physicians for medical malpractice. Of course, the physician plaintiff will generally require more blatant provocation, but if he or his family is the victim of clear negligence the injured doctor will rarely hesitate to sue his colleague.

Those who would ban malpractice litigation assert that medicine is a vital service essential to the public welfare and must not be subject to the usual civil law. This viewpoint, shared by many medical practitioners, falters under close scrutiny. Is it really true that medicine is any more vital or special than any other public service? The answer, I believe, is no.

The American public has come to equate good health with medical care. There is a relationship, but medical care is only one small component of personal health. Health is an innate, natural quality subject to predetermined genetic factors, environmental controls, and some medical modification. Medicine may intervene, but its powers relative to those of natural and environmental determinants are limited.

There are many public services which are of more pressing daily import than medical care. Consider the disruption and public threat when there is a garbage-collection strike, a truckers' stoppage, a power failure, or an airline strike. There would be far more immediate and devastating hardship, disease, and death if food stores suddenly had empty shelves, if the city's water supply became depleted or contaminated, if all electrical power failed, or if all gasoline supplies were abruptly terminated, than if all medical services ground to a sudden halt. True, without physicians and hospital services some people would die, but without food, water, power, or transportation all of us would die, and far more quickly.

For a physician to assert that he should be immune from legal acton because he provides a vital service is, therefore, untenable. One could muster as strong an argument to support the food packer whose botulism-contaminated canned soup killed ten people. He provides a vital service—food supplying. In fact, his wide national market serves many more people than the small practice of a single physician. The food packer must be accountable for his error, and so must the doctor.

Medical practitioners do not deserve special favors, but they do deserve equal protection under the law. Those who are asking for special consideration for doctors have a point, but the valid justification is not that doctors are a privileged group, but rather that they have been singled out as targets for legal harassment. Suits against doctors far exceed those against members of any other groups. Many claims are valid, but many are brought by patients anxious to vent their anger on a prime target or eager to make a quick dollar. Physicians must be shielded from this exploitation. Because they have become unique victims of our legal system, some special changes should be made to protect them, while carefully ensuring continued accountability.

Proper solutions must maintain the public right to legal redress at the same time as they deal with the most pressing excesses of bias against the medical community. The voluminous wave of nonmeritorious suits and the inordinately high awards in successful ones must be brought under control. Preliminary screening panels and legislated upper limits for monetary awards may alleviate some of these problems, but in the final analysis, legal recourse should be reserved for those cases in which fundamental rights have truly been violated.